SYNODALITY

SYNODALITY

A New Way of Proceeding in the Church

Rafael Luciani

Paulist Press
New York / Mahwah, NJ

Cover image by Lightspring/Shutterstock.com
Cover design by Sharyn Banks
Book design by Lynn Else

Translated from the Spanish for Paulist Press by Joseph Owens, SJ. Copyright © 2022 by Rafael Luciani
Foreword by Peter Hünermann was translated into English by Yeshica Marianne Umaña Calderón.

Library of Congress Cataloging-in-Publication Data
Names: Luciani, Rafael, author.
Title: Synodality : a new way of proceeding in the church / Rafael Luciani ; translated by Joseph Owens, SJ.
Other titles: Sinodalidad. English
Description: New York ; Mahwah : Paulist Press, [2022] | Includes bibliographical references. | Summary: "Synodality as a new way of proceeding in the Church: towards a co-responsible and participatory Church for the Third Millennium"—Provided by publisher.
Identifiers: LCCN 2021048848 (print) | LCCN 2021048849 (ebook) | ISBN 9780809156115 (paperback) | ISBN 9780809187713 (ebook)
Subjects: LCSH: Church renewal—Catholic Church. | Catholic Church—Government.
Classification: LCC BX1746 .L93713 2022 (print) | LCC BX1746 (ebook) | DDC 262/.02—dc23/eng/20220110
LC record available at https://lccn.loc.gov/2021048848
LC ebook record available at https://lccn.loc.gov/2021048849

ISBN 978-0-8091-5611-5 (paperback)
ISBN 978-0-8091-8771-3 (e-book)

Published by Paulist Press
997 Macarthur Boulevard
Mahwah, New Jersey 07430
www.paulistpress.com

Printed and bound in the
United States of America

CONTENTS

Foreword by Peter Hünermann vii

Abbreviations...xv

Introduction 1

Part I: From Pastoral Conversion to Synodal Conversion..... 5

1. An Institutional Failure?.. 7
   An Obstacle to Discovering the Gospel 7
   Clericalism and Ecclesial Power.................................... 9
   The Systemic Problem of an Ecclesiological Model................... 11

2. Renewal and Reform through Pastoral Conversion 15
   Ecclesia semper reformanda...................................... 15
   Abandoning Outdated Structures 18
   The Path of Pastoral Conversion................................... 22

3. Introducing Synodality.. 26
   A New Ecclesial Model 26
   An Ecclesial Way of Proceeding 28

4. Synodality and Decision-Making................................... 33
   The Whole Community 33
   The Synodal Process of Decision-Making 36

CONTENTS

Part II: Synodality and the People of God 43

5. The People of God as All the Faithful 45
   Recovering the Normative Character of the People of God 45
   We Are All *Christifideles* 50

6. Reciprocity and Respectivity 58
   The Priesthood of the Faithful and the Ordained Ministry 58
   Episcopal Collegiality and Primacy 62

7. Ecclesiogenesis 70
   The Expansion of Episcopal Collegiality 71
   The Laity as a Subject 79

8. The Challenge of Synodal Ecclesiality 87
   Linking *sensus fidei* and *consensus omnium fidelium* 87
   The Sociocultural Dynamics of the *sensus populi* 96

Part III: Synodality and the Local Churches 103

9. The Local Church 105
   The Eclipse of the Ecclesiology of Local Churches 107
   Recovering the "Catholicity" of Local Churches 110
   Ecclesiology as *Ecclesiogenesis* 112

10. The Latin American Church—a Case Study 117
    A New Way of Being Church 118
       Synodality Broadens and Completes Collegiality 118
       Synodality as Listening and Consulting 122
       Synodality as Discernment and Dialogue 127
       Synodality as Unity and Diversity 131
    New Spirit, New Structures 134

Conclusion: "A More Complete Definition of the Church" 139

Notes 147

Selected Bibliography 175

FOREWORD

Peter Hünermann

The theological reflections and the appeals for the realization of synodality that were expressed or presented after the Second Vatican Council, and especially by Pope Francis himself, have not yet led to a major breakthrough. From the beginning of his pontificate, Pope Francis has repeatedly referred to synodality, and his speech commemorating the fiftieth anniversary of the Synod of Bishops on October 17, 2015, was particularly striking. The pope emphasized at the outset that he had endeavored to value the Synod from the very beginning of his ministry as Bishop of Rome. He presents the thesis: "The path of synodality is the path that God expects of His Church in the third millennium."

In this address, Pope Francis impressively explains from the New Testament how the people of God—according to the texts of the Second Vatican Council—are not simply to be understood as a passive "receiving" subject, but as an active, responsible subject of evangelization. It is an absurdity to distinguish rigidly between *ecclesia docens* and *ecclesia discens*, between a teaching and a learning Church. Therefore, the bishops are obliged to listen carefully to the people of God, just as the people of God are obliged to listen to the voice of the bishops. In doing so, the pope in no way diminishes the special task of the bishops to care for the unity and *conspiratio* of the many (*Lumen Gentium* 18).

In listening to one another, it is essentially a matter of "listening to God": with God the outcry of the people is to be heard, the will to breathe, to which God calls us. This also applies to Peter as well as to the pope because the Synod must always act "with Peter and under Peter"—not as a limitation of freedom, but also as a guarantee of unity. From this, it follows that a synodal Church must be characterized by a dynamic of communion that should reflect all ecclesial decisions. This is transferred by the pope to all levels of ecclesial life, and especially the bishops' conferences.

Here a quiet urgent question arises: What is wrong with the Church, with the bishops, but also with canonists and theologians, if one sees that in the Episcopal Conference among practical theologians and canonists no fundamental approaches show up to put these challenges into practice? What are the reasons why there has been little change in the Church order until now?

This critical question in no way denies that there have been processes of consultation and discussion in many dioceses in recent years. For the most part, they have not been carried out in the form envisaged by canon law, because here there are very many provisions that are so restrictive that, in most cases, the holding of such diocesan synods has led to considerable frustration on the part of the participating laypeople, the synodal members. If one asks about the reasons for the given precarious situation of the Church, one must first recall the nature of the Church. In his remarks on the nature of the Catholic Church, Walter Kasper says,

Foreword

> [The] Church is … the space of salvation given by God,
> and in this deeper theological sense really a "divine"
> institution. Its concrete realization, however, happens
> in a historical way. This is ultimately due to the fact
> that the acceptance of salvation is in its essence a free
> human act. The permanent essential structures of the
> church are thus always realized in contingent expres-
> sions of time and cultural history, which must not be
> absolutized. Hence, we have the unchangeable *ius divi-
> num* only in changeable *ius humanum*. In this respect,
> even a theological justification of law has anthropo-
> logical presuppositions. Concretely formulated: As a
> divine institution, the church must at the same time be
> an institution of human and Christian freedom and, as
> such, have a model character.[1]

If this description of the nature of the Church is adequate,
what are the concrete reasons and obstacles that stand in the way of
such a Church described? Based on John XXIII's remarks regarding the *signs of the times* and the invocation of this criterion, Pope
Francis has deepened and operationalized the use of these *signs of
the times* in his assessments of social situations and positions.

To assess this historical situation, the pope does not call
for more detailed sociological and related studies. This usually
leads to a "diagnostic overhang that is not always accompanied
by truly applicable proposals for solutions" (*Evangelii Gaudium*
50). Rather, he asks about current "trends" in the present situation that, if they do not find good solutions, trigger processes of
dehumanization that are very difficult to reverse. In view of such
signs and indications, in the situations themselves, "it is appropriate to clarify what can be a fruit of God's kingdom and also what
is detrimental to God's plan" (*EG* 51).

If one follows these criteria, then the leading question is, What are the greatest abuses, the greatest scandals, that have most deeply injured the relationship of trust, the willingness of the people to believe, and the credibility of the faith community of the Church? The answer: the sexual abuse and the financial scandals of the Church. The outrage against sexual abuse in the Church does not refer to the fact that such abuse actually exists. There are similar cases in numerous other social environments. The indignation is mainly directed at the fact that Church superiors, bishops, and religious superiors did not punish these abuses appropriately, but rather made them a taboo and often covered them up. The victims were not acknowledge in an effort to keep the reputation of the Church and the clergy "spotless" and "holy." That this was a widespread practice was shown by the major disclosure processes in Ireland, Australia, and now in Chile and Germany.

This is an outrageous, inhumane practice that grew out of the "habitual practice" of the leading clergy. This practice was made possible because there is no independent system of justice in the Church, no independent process of legislation and prosecution. The bishop—like the religious superior—is the leader[2] and thus he unites executive, judicative, and legislative power in his sphere of authority. The governor is his own judge and controller. This conception is reminiscent of the constitutional form of small absolutist principalities in the eighteenth century. The Code of Canon Law protects this conception at the level of the whole Church through primacy.

In the case of financial scandals, the people of God are outraged that the money donated by the faithful for the purposes of the gospel is illegitimately exploited for private enrichment or collected through a church tax. This is also about the lack of independent and therefore transparent control of the dioceses, of the money received, and the corresponding financing of the commitments made by the Church, such as the employment of pastoral personnel, the maintenance and management of public ecclesiastical works committed to the Church and to the public good. The complexity of public budgets with debts, investments in the future, and liabilities is also reflected in the budgets of church institutions. To protect this highly complex financial situation from selfish arbitrariness and to make and maintain it serviceable for the common good, modern society is faced with the continuous task of perfecting its legislation as well as its administrative, control, and security measures.

What is the situation in the Church? The property law of the Church has been oriented—since about the sixth century—essentially to a multitude of legal entities, the dioceses, parishes, monasteries, foundations, benefices, and so on, that is, the ecclesiastical legal persons who have legally acquired the property. It is based on the strict earmarking of church property and thus establishes the Church's independent right to property and its independent administration. A holistic concept of governance is always assumed, which does not recognize any functional diversification. This aspect is not taken up in modern canon law.

What is very much absent from the forty-six canons of the 1983 Code of Canon Law—as in the much more comprehensive 1917 Code of Canon Law—is the responsibility of ecclesiastical authority to shape the public law framework that can ensure the earmarking of ecclesiastical goods and the earmarking of governance and administration according to the spirit of the gospel in modern times.

Synodality—the involvement of the people of God as an active subject in the fundamental decision-making processes of the Church—is a process of profound transformation in today's Church and in today's social situation. Synodality offers the only way out of the series of scandals. If the *ius divinum* can occur only in the form of the *ius humanum*, and therefore the Church as a divine institution is at the same time an institution of human and Christian freedom, and as such should have a model character, then it is necessary to initiate a reform that concerns the ecclesiastical understanding of office and governance in forms of life and law that are apparently divinely sanctioned by ecclesiastical tradition. Synodality requires independent, autonomous, and creative forms of legislation that are based on ecclesiastical and theological tradition.

Only by bringing about such functional independence and autonomy in the Church is the Church, as a body founded by revelation, in a position, today, to be manageable, functional, credible, and trustworthy. The scandals cited, and that continue, indicate this sufficiently. Synodality does not mean simply adopting political democracy and adapting to the spirit of the times. It is about the dignity of the people of God and the human form that allows the preservation of this dignity in modern society.

How can such a process be initiated? Steps must be taken at all levels: of the parishes and deaneries; of dioceses; of episcopal conferences; of united patriarchates; of continents; and finally, at the level of the whole Church. It is true that the real introduction of synodal structures cannot simply be "from above" because the differences in the various nations, cultural areas, and continents must be considered. It is important, however, to set the general goals from the top, but then to start the real construction from the bottom. Sufficient space will have to be given to the preparatory phase. Time is needed to prepare the people of God, to prepare the personnel. Parallel to this, the regulations in force must be handled in a "relaxed manner" in accordance with the new objectives.

The hub for the first phase, which refers to the dioceses and parishes or deaneries, is likely to be the level of the Conference of Bishops. Regarding specifically the level of the bishops' conference, as such, it cannot carry out these decisions in realizing synodality independently of competent laypersons and the consultation of various experts. The aim is that this process should create the conditions for a national synodal constitution, which would establish the church order in the sphere of the Conference of Bishops and set the framework for an independent judiciary and executive.

The Statute of the Common Synod of Dioceses in the Federal Republic of Germany, confirmed by Rome for the implementation of the Würzburg Synod 1971–75, can be used here as a model. The statute provides for the right to vote on all decisions for all Synod members. The German bishops, as a college, have a right of veto. For "reasons of the binding doctrine of faith and morals of the Church," they could declare a decision of the Synod's plenary assembly "impossible." "A renewed referral of the question to the competent commission for the elaboration of a new one is thus not excluded."[3] Because of the different numbers of Synod members to be elected from the different groups (priests, laity, religious men and women), and the different groups entitled to vote (dioceses: priests' and diocesan councils; Central Committee of German Catholics: Catholic associations; religious: Association of Major Superiors), the structure of the Joint Synod resembled in a certain way the Anglican synod structure.

Only from such initial drafts and trials can the next steps be taken regarding the levels of the major cultural areas of the continents and the universal Church. One can clearly see, here, the challenges the Catholic Church is facing today. This whole process, which is highly necessary, is likely to take a considerable amount of time. It is a task that requires all the powers and gifts of the Spirit.

In this sense, Rafael Luciani's book will contribute to reflect on and deepen these questions so that the objective proposed by Pope Francis, in accordance with the teachings of the Second Vatican Council, becomes a reality in the life of our churches, because "the path of synodality is the path that God expects of His Church in the third millennium."

ABBREVIATIONS

AA	*Apostolicam Actuositatem*
AG	*Ad Gentes*
AS	*Apostolos Suos*
CIC	*Codex Iuris Canonici*
DF	Final Document of the Synod for the Pan-Amazonian Region
DV	*Dei Verbum*
EC	*Episcopalis Communio*
EG	*Evangelii Gaudium*
EN	*Evangelii Nuntiandi*
GS	*Gaudium et Spes*
IDS	Instruction of Diocesan Synods, *De synodis dioecesanis agendis*
IL	*Instrumentum Laboris*
ITC	International Theological Commission
LG	*Lumen Gentium*
PNE	Preliminary Note of Explanation
PO	*Presbyterorum Ordinis*
QA	*Querida Amazonia*
UR	*Unitatis Redintegratio*

INTRODUCTION

The search for a new institutional model of the Church for this new millennium cannot forget the words that Pope Paul VI addressed to the Roman curia on September 21, 1963, inviting us to receive the Council with a spirit of *perennis reformatio* (perpetual reformation). But, as noted during his opening speech at Vatican II's second session, held a few days later on September 29, 1963, "This reform pays homage to tradition by seeking to strip away all its outdated and defective manifestations in order to render it genuine and fruitful," and, he added, that this task presupposes the "desire, the need, and the duty of the Church finally to provide a more complete definition of itself."

This was not a call for a mere act of an administrative reorganization of the Church. At stake was the Church's fidelity to her calling as follower of Jesus and her response to the new signs of the times. Therefore, a true and permanent reform, as proposed by the Second Vatican Council, should always consider the search for a new ecclesial way of proceeding to bring about an ecclesiological change that affects not only the very identity and mission of the institution, but also the way in which the Church defines the identities and relationships of all the ecclesial subjects, and how the communicative dynamics within the structures are understood.

With this spirit, the pontificate of Francis has inaugurated a new phase in the reception of Vatican II, one rooted in the ecclesiology of the people of God, understanding the normativity of chapter 2 of *Lumen Gentium* in the process of reconfiguring the whole Church. Francis has expressed this through his many words, gestures, and deeds. However, it is specifically during the Commemoration of the 50th Anniversary of the Institution of the Synod of Bishops that the pope proposed a new way of proceeding in the Church that will lead to a new ecclesiological model. He calls it a "synodal Church," and states that "a synodal Church is a Church that listens, with the understanding that listening 'is more than hearing.' It is reciprocal listening in which everyone has something to learn."

Listening cannot be understood as a simple act. It is not hearing. Listening becomes a communicative dynamic that redefines and reconfigures the identities and relationships among all the faithful or ecclesial subjects in which the whole people of God—pope, bishops, laity, and so on—take part. Therefore, listening characterizes the entire process of interaction and connection that occurs among all of them: "Faithful people, episcopal college, Bishop of Rome: each one listening to the others, and all listening to the Holy Spirit, the 'Spirit of Truth' (John 14:17), to know what he 'is telling the churches' (Rev 2:7)." In this reciprocal and horizontal dynamic, the teaching body not only listens to the people of God, but it listens as part of the people of God (cf. *DV* 10). In this new model, the hierarchy must be at the service of the rest of the faithful, being and acting as one of the faithful within the whole people of God.

In a synodal Church, we are asked not only to walk together —a simplistic way to understand synodality—but rather, and above all, it highlights the relations and the communicative dynamics happening while walking together. It involves the dynamic of praying, meeting, and working together, but also of discerning, and making, and taking decisions together. It is a new ecclesial culture of taking advice and building consensus. By doing so, we can overcome the pyramidal and clericalist model of a Church that teaches and another one that learns and follows. A synodal model involves the entire ecclesial community to seek new ways of proceeding as one people of God living in a multiform and polyhedron communion.

Synodality is a constitutive and constituent dimension of the life and mission of the Church. Therefore, it requires the constant reassessment of lifestyles, discernment practices, and governance structures. We can speak of a conversion of the mentalities, implying to rethink the relations of authority and equality, and so advance toward a new ecclesial way of proceeding grounded in the base that encompasses all the faithful who make up the people of God. Such synodality is a new mark of the Church, a mode of being and operating that affects the Church's life, its ways of understanding and practicing discernment, and the ways it functions, with implications in governance, and especially such topics as participation and accountability.

Regardless, we should not confuse synodality with synods. We cannot treat synodality simply as a concept derived from collegiality or conciliarity. It is not just a specific event nor a functional method. It is a constitutive dimension that qualifies ecclesiality and defines a new way of proceeding for the Church as people of God. Thus, it invites her to re-form by reconfiguring her into an ecclesial "we," where all subjects, from the pope to the laity, are equals and articulated in a communion of faithful with the same responsibility regarding the identity, vocation, and mission of the Church.

For many Catholics, even in the academy, it is difficult to understand synodality not just as a way of enhancing processes of consultation and listening in the Church, without realizing the implications that it has for a permanent reform of the Church and for the way in which theology is done today. Synodality affects not only mentalities that need to be converted and updated, but also structures and relationships among all ecclesial subjects, and at all levels, from bishops to laity, from parishes to the curia, and from base communities to the academy. The newness of the current ecclesial epoch is that the Church is in transition, one in which reform is understood as a permanent process, so that ecclesiology becomes *ecclesiogenesis*, and where the theological and the pastoral cannot be separated, or else ecclesial life and theological reflection may become an ideology, an abstract thought without transcendence and reality for the people, to whom all the faithful are called to serve as one.

Advances have been made: Vatican II proposed an episcopal collegiality; Francis has proposed a collegial synodality, especially through the Synod of Bishops; and currently, the Latin American Church is giving birth to an ecclesial synodality. This book offers some key basic elements of synodality and presents how this new way of proceeding might emerge in the global Church, stemming from a more comprehensive reception of the ecclesiology of the people of God.

It is precisely through synodality that the Church manifests and reconfigures herself as people of God in a continual and communal process of ecclesiogenesis, that is, a perpetual state of conversion and reform. We are therefore faced with the challenge of deepening a synodal ecclesiality, a new theological-cultural institutional model of Church for the third millennium, and, moreover, the synodalization of the whole Church. Maybe we are at the crossroads of having found an ecclesial model that responds to what Pope Paul VI called "a more complete definition of the Church." That is what synodality represents today and the challenge that the Church of the third millennium faces.

PART I

FROM PASTORAL CONVERSION TO SYNODAL CONVERSION

1

An Institutional Failure?

AN OBSTACLE TO
DISCOVERING THE GOSPEL

Today, we find ourselves at a crossroads. We are experiencing a crisis in the transmission of the faith, a crisis caused by the continued existence of a *clerical institutional model*. We are still dealing with "*a clerical and authoritarian church that is torn apart by the conflict* between groups with a renewed awareness and traditional groups with their established structures."[1] In this context, we must ask, What must be reformed? Several diverse factors are at the root of the present crisis, and they must be considered as a whole, not in isolation.

Long before the Council, Yves Congar expressed that the crisis in which we find ourselves is "that of a particular Christian civilization, a certain Christian world, a certain Christian mentality—ultimately, a crisis of sociological structures that represent, not Christian reality, but rather *a certain concrete expression of the way things are done*."[2] Therefore, any process of reform must begin by distinguishing between that which is permanent and

that which is always subject to reform. As the visionary Domini-
can theologian explained,

> Christianity is eternal, but the *forms* in which it is
> expressed and currently embodied in Christian civi-
> lization, the actual organization of its apostolic life,
> the universal and local administrative structure of the
> church, even the celebration of worship and certain
> elements of the Christian philosophy of man and of
> society—all these in great part are linked to history
> and conditioned by a given stage of development.
> To desire to ascribe the value and the permanence
> of all these things to Christianity itself would mean
> absolutizing what is actually relative. This is a kind of
> idolatry related to the mistake of relativizing what is
> absolute....I want to clarify the distinction and the
> connection between what is permanently valuable and
> what by its nature can become obsolete.[3]

Congar was referring to a *model of institutionality* that
needed to be reformed because it had created and empowered an
ecclesial culture and an institutional way of proceeding characterized by *clericalism*.

In his work *Nueva conciencia de la Iglesia en América Latina*
[New awareness of the Church in Latin America], written after
the Council, one of Latin America's most important ecclesiolo-
gists, Ronaldo Muñoz, stressed the Council's call for reform not
only of ecclesial mentalities but also of *ecclesial structures*. In 1972,
Muñoz warned that "the *clerical institution* is one of the great *structural obstacles* to discovering the Gospel."[4] Because he understood
the clericalization of the institution as a systemic problem, he proposed that the Church should "reform its internal relations and

institutions."[5] If the institution's historical form—theological-cultural model—is the means by which the memory[6] of the faith is (or is not) communicated in each epoch, then the Church is *always in need of reform*. The call made by these two theologians to reform a clericalized institutional model of the Church speak to the current circumstances.

CLERICALISM AND ECCLESIAL POWER

Today, various international studies have confirmed the diagnosis and analysis of these two great theologians from very different continents, concluding that the Church has a *systemic* problem. Two recent studies shed light on our reflection: (a) the *Final Report* of the Royal Commission into Institutional Responses to Child Sexual Abuse,[7] which was set up by the Australian government to study the period 1950 to 2017; and (b) the report on "Sexual Abuse of Minors by Priests, Deacons, and Male Religious in the Area of the German Bishops' Conference between 1946 and 2014," commissioned by the German Bishop's Conference and published in 2018.[8] The Australian report declared,

> If one had to isolate one single factor that has contributed to the toxic response of Catholic Church leaders to victims of sexual abuse it would be clericalism…. Clericalism is a virus that has infected the Church, or any church, whereby it is believed that the churchmen, the priests, the bishops, are in some form or way sacred and above ordinary people, and because of this sacredness, because of their importance, they must be held as more important and be more protected.[9]

Both these studies, undertaken by interdisciplinary teams, agree that the problem of clericalism has to do with the conception and the exercise of power and authority in the Church. The Australian commission states, "The deepest questions to be addressed at all levels in the Church are around the malaise of clericalism with its misunderstanding of power and authority and the specialness of ordination."[10] Such a diagnosis agrees closely with the analysis that Pope Francis has been making. During his apostolic journey to Mozambique and Madagascar, Francis told the Jesuits, "Clericalism is a true perversion in the Church....Clericalism condemns, separates, frustrates, and despises the people of God."[11] And he told the Synod of Bishops in 2018, "It is necessary to overcome decisively the plague of clericalism....Clericalism is a perversion and the root of many evils in the Church. We must humbly ask to be forgiven for them, and we must above all create the conditions not to repeat them."[12]

Among the factors contributing to the consolidation of an ecclesial clerical culture are the theology of ordained ministry, the present ecclesiological model, the exercise of power and leadership in the hierarchy, celibacy and the culture of secrecy, the theology of forgiveness, and the work environment in ecclesial structures. All these factors share a common element that lies at the base of the problem: "The relation between power and impotence in the clerical and hierarchical system of the Catholic Church, along with the idea of an ontological change at ordination."[13] The pope uses a very forceful expression: "the complex of being chosen."[14] He is referring to the origin of what he calls the "pathology of ecclesial power."

Clericalism develops and flourishes in the formation houses of seminarians, and male and women religious. It extends to the parishes and the laity and is strengthened with lifestyles that are not in accord with the prophetic dimension of ecclesial ministry. Francis criticizes those who understand the call to priesthood or religious life in terms of a deformed theology of "being chosen." According to such a theology, God separates certain persons from the world and grants them a higher status with respect to other members of the Church.[15] In this way ordained ministry and the clerical institution are *sacralized*; "priestly *service* is confused with priestly power.... Ministry is understood not as service but as *promotion to the altar.*"[16]

The German report also recognizes that "clericalism denotes a hierarchical, authoritarian system that can lead priests to adopt a dominating attitude in relating to non-ordained individuals because they occupy a superior position by virtue of their ministry and ordination."[17] It is possible, therefore, to speak of a whole clerical culture in which priests form part of an institutional model that is monarchical in practice and socially stratified. The very nature of such a structure has created a "clerical aristocracy" that is expressed in lifestyles and clothing as well as in relations of power and obedience that are graded and never horizontal.[18]

A study published in Latin America by CEPROME (Center for Interdisciplinary Research and Formation for the Protection of Minors in Mexico) corroborates this finding. It maintains that in the Church's present institutional crisis "clericalism is an important element to consider in trying to understand both the distortion of the power exercised over persons by the cleric who is called to serve and, at the institutional level, the distortion of the power exercised by the hierarchy over the people of God."[19]

THE SYSTEMIC PROBLEM OF AN ECCLESIOLOGICAL MODEL

We are faced with an ecclesial culture that needs reform; we are dealing with a "state of things," not simply individual actions or isolated instances of abuse in the exercise of power. And since it is an ecclesial culture, it affects everything and everybody in the Church because "there are attitudinal, behavioral, and institutional dimensions to the phenomenon of clericalism."[20] In other words,

> Clericalism arises from both personal and social dynamics, is expressed in various cultural forms, and often is reinforced by institutional structures. Among its chief manifestations are an authoritarian style of ministerial leadership, a rigidly hierarchical worldview, and a virtual identification of the holiness and grace of the church with the clerical state and, thereby, with the cleric himself.[21]

Theologian Eamonn Conway argues that this situation forces us to consider the possibility of "institutional failure."[22] The problems concern not only organizational forms and technical procedures in the Church, which are mentioned also in a study commissioned by the United States Catholic Conference of Bishops,[23] but above all an *ecclesiological model* whose theological and cultural bases are in crisis, making it clear that the ecclesial structure "has a problem with power."[24] Jörg Fegert and Michael Kölch assert that these problems cannot be attributed to the bad conduct of individuals, something that can be corrected; rather, we are faced with the failure of the Church's present *institutional form.*[25] Thus, as the German bishops point out, "the failure of the institution that does not protect victims" is directly related to the abuse of power in the Church, specifically sexual abuse.[26]

Consequently, if "the problem is systemic and [exists] in every part of the Catholic Church at the international level,"[27] if it adheres to a Constantinian ecclesiology[28] that defines an ontologically unequal society, and if it "gives rise to a dual model of Church in which the Church of the clergy is superior and more 'holy' when compared with the Church of the laity,"[29] then the question is this: How do we build a new institutional model that is not clericalized? The answer necessarily involves the *conversion of the hierarchical institution*. In accordance with the spirit and the letter of Vatican II, this means situating collegiality and primacy within the people of God, not vice versa, with the objective of forging a new ecclesial way of proceeding that implies the conversion of mentalities and the reform of structures.

The Spanish Benedictine Lluis Duch used to speak of the need to recover *structures of acceptance* that can mediate human relations and forge creative links between past, present, and future.[30] Regarding the Church, however, Ronaldo Muñoz stressed that it needs to become

> a community of free and open persons who cooperate responsibly. The Church should be a community in which all unite in solidarity and participate actively in an attitude of ongoing searching and self-criticism. At all levels there should be *structures of participation* for lay people, religious, and priests and the possibility of choosing the representatives and leaders. The hierarchy should consult the laity regarding their pastoral decisions and their declarations. The hierarchy should trust more in the maturity of the laity, especially working-class folk, and should recognize in practice the autonomy of initiative and movement that corresponds to the laity in temporal affairs. The priests, religious, and active laity of the local church should participate in the naming of the bishop.[31]

In this beautiful, though challenging description of *ecclesiality*, we can find the emergence of a synodal Church. Latin America's ecclesial reception of the Second Vatican Council took place originally in 1968 at Medellín, the Second Latin American Episcopal Conference, which proclaimed the Church as the people of God in the midst of all the peoples of this earth (*LG* 13), truly a *Church of churches* (*LG* 23).

2

Renewal and Reform through Pastoral Conversion

ECCLESIA SEMPER REFORMANDA

Advancing the call of the Second Vatican Council to "reform" the Church (*Unitatis Redintegratio* 4.6), Pope Francis has made clear that "Christ calls the pilgrim Church to *perennial reform*" (*Evangelii Gaudium* 26),[1] understood as the convergence of two mutually related processes: *pastoral* and *synodal conversions*. The relation between these two notions explains the *ecclesiogenesis* to which we are now transitioning. *Pastoral conversion* represents the genuinely Latin American root of the Council's reception, while *synodal conversion* represents the deepening of the text and the spirit of the event of the Council.

It is in this context that Francis's call for a reform of the Church is to be understood. During the Eucharist celebrated in Santa Marta on November 9, 2013, Francis stated, "*Ecclesia semper reformanda.* The Church always needs to be renewed because its members are sinners and need *conversion.*"[2] In other words, he understands Church reform not as a one-time act of revision or as the updating of certain outdated structures, but as a constant, permanent process of *ecclesial conversion* involving *the whole Church*. He confirmed this conception on November 24, 2013, when he issued his apostolic exhortation *Evangelii Gaudium*, the document that would serve as his road map:

> Paul VI invited us to deepen the call to renewal so as to make plain that renewal concerns not only individuals but the entire Church....The Second Vatican Council presented ecclesial conversion as an openness to constant self-renewal born of fidelity to Jesus Christ....Christ summons the Church, as she goes her pilgrim way...to that continual reformation of which she always has need. (*EG* 26)

One year later, in 2014, he presented a brief phenomenological description of the unhealthy elements in contemporary ecclesial culture that needed to be reformed. He spoke of neglect of controls, excessive planning and functionalism, loss of communion among members of the ecclesial body, extravagant garments and honors, careerism and opportunism, and membership in closed circles.[3] In his discourse, he stressed particular aspects of lifestyles, discernment practices, and governance structures.

In 2015, the pope spoke of the *service* of collaboration between the universal Church and local churches, and he insisted on *professionalism* to ensure better functioning of Church government. He then added a third element that was "*the basis of the quality* of our work," namely, "direct contact with God's people,"[4] especially the poorest. In this regard, Francis pointed out that the meaning of *reform* is twofold: first, it should "*con-form* to the Good News that must be proclaimed to all with courage and joy, and especially to the poor, the marginalized, and the outcast"; and second, it should also "*con-form* to the signs of our times." He insisted that the curia should *con-form*, which is to collaborate with the specific ministry of the successor of the Apostle Peter, "so that they may better meet the needs of the men and women whom they are called to serve."[5]

By relating Church reform to the Church's mission in the world, and in turn, relating this mission to human needs, especially those of the poor, Francis shows a clear continuity with Paul VI, who, during the last public session of the Council, elucidated the Council's spirit by alluding to the Good Samaritan,[6] a figure to whom Francis often refers. In 2003, ten years before being elected pope, the then-Cardinal Bergoglio used the parable of the Good Samaritan during the *Te Deum* celebrated in the Cathedral of Buenos Aires to propose the image of a Church in exit (*Iglesia en salida*) that defines herself by serving the wounded people.[7] The Church's efforts must therefore promote and accompany "decisions, programs, mechanisms, and processes specifically geared to a better distribution of income, the creation of sources of employment, and an integral promotion of the poor which goes beyond a simple welfare mentality" (*EG* 204).

Following this train of thought, we can see that, for Francis, "reform is not an end in itself, but rather a process of growth and above all of *conversion*." He insists,

> Reform will be effective if and only if it is carried out with "renewed" persons and not simply with "new"

men and women occupying positions in a Church that has not yet converted in her structures. It is not enough only to change personnel; the members of the Curia must be led to *renew themselves spiritually, personally, and professionally.* Reform of the Curia does not come about with a simple change of persons—which undoubtedly happens and will continue to happen—but with *the conversion of persons.* In reality, "permanent formation" is not enough; rather, "permanent conversion and purification" are above all necessary. *Without a "change of mentality" a dutiful effort will be useless.*[8]

ABANDONING OUTDATED STRUCTURES

Francis envisions *pastoral conversion* as the way the process of "perennial reform" (*EG* 26) will take place:

I dream of a "missionary option," that is, a missionary impulse capable of transforming everything, so that the Church's customs, ways of doing things, times and schedules, language and structures can be suitably channeled for the evangelization of today's world rather than for her self-preservation. The renewal of structures demanded by pastoral conversion can be understood only in this light: as part of an effort to make them more mission-oriented, to make ordinary pastoral activity on every level more inclusive and open, to inspire in pastoral workers a constant desire to go forth and in this way to elicit a positive response from all those whom Jesus summons to friendship with him. (*EG* 27)

Thus, pastoral conversion is presented as a *sine qua non* of real ecclesial reform. That means modifying "customs, ways of doing things, times and schedules, language and structures" and feeling a "constant desire to go forth" into the world. In fact, pastoral conversion is clearly necessary because "all renewal in the Church must have mission as its goal if it is not to fall prey to a kind of ecclesial introversion" (*EG* 27).[9] Here we find a key element, as he stated during his speech to the cardinals prior to the conclave, when he argued that "the Church is called to move out of itself and advance to the peripheries." The change is not merely one of social place; it is also a change of *hermeneutical* space, which allows the Church to engage with the world and so discern its identity and mission in light of the signs of the times.

Francis's vision of the peripheries finds its ecclesiological roots in what Cardinal Suenens referred to after the Council, when speaking about the need to overcome the pyramidal and hierarchical model of preconciliar times. The cardinal used the metaphor of *two ways of looking*. The first way referred to the approach where "the common direction of the gaze looks *from the center toward the periphery*." The second, in contrast, was to be found in the "approach that looks *from the periphery toward the center*."[10] Adopting this metaphor, we can say that Francis is not concerned with finding new methods for a more effective announcement of the kerygma; he is concerned, rather, with initiating processes of constant personal conversion and structural reforms that will involve a *permanent attitude of going forth to the peripheries*. After going forth to the peripheries, the return to the center involves a conversion, an ecclesial way of proceeding in which a call is issued from the base to reestablish a universal communion of all subjects at all levels so that we are constituted the people of God. With this mindset, there cannot be bishops or priests without the people of God; they too are so many sheep in the flock.

This *going forth*—the fruit of pastoral conversion—is not a particular act but a *permanent state of mission* (*EG* 25) among the peoples of this earth (*EG* 115). This going forth makes it possible for the founding event of Christianity to be continually updated and renewed, because it reinterprets Christian tradition in the light of each new sociocultural context in which the mission takes place, always in a reciprocal relationship with those receiving the announcement. Rather than stressing just doctrinal or thematic matters, it is important to give priority to the cultural aspects of communicating and implementing the Church's mission in the world (*AG* 10–11). Reforms are carried out from below, based on decisions and processes in the local churches; they are then referred upward.

One may think that the notion of pastoral conversion means merely a new pastoral plan for our times or a renewed model of evangelization, but that is incorrect. Its origin is found in the *Fourth General Conference of the Bishops of Latin America and the Caribbean* held in *Santo Domingo* in 1992. It was defined there as follows:

> The New Evangelization requires *pastoral conversion* of the Church. Such conversion must be in keeping with the Council. It touches everything and everyone; it relates to conscience and also to personal and community practice; it involves relations of equality and authority; it requires structures and dynamics that make the Church ever more clearly present as an effective sign, as the sacrament of universal salvation. (*SD* 30)

This text points to a deepening of the Council's ecclesiology. Regarding a conversion of mentalities, it asks for a rethinking of the Church's mission—both in what it is and what it does. This rethinking is referred to as a conversion of *consciousness* and of *praxis*. According to the spirit of the text, the change will be verified concretely in the exercise of *authority*, and specifically when authority is exercised in light of the relations of *equality* that emerge from the *sensus fidelium*.

On this basis, the bishops seek the conversion of *structures* through the creation of internal *dynamics* or processes that favor more effective fulfillment of the Church's mission in the world. Thus, the *Santo Domingo* document presents the notion of pastoral conversion as an organic, structuring principle governing all ecclesial genesis and organization; it affects "everything and everyone" as regards lifestyles (personal and community practice), exercise of authority and power (relations of equality and authority), and ecclesial models (structures and dynamics). Its implementation supposes policies to overcome clericalism, because it touches the very nature of the crisis—the notion and the exercise of power and authority in the Church—that calls for a reform of some theologies of ordained ministry not yet aligned with the Council.

The Latin American tradition continued and deepened this path, in 2007, at the *Fifth General Conference of the Bishops of Latin America and the Caribbean* held in Aparecida. The call for pastoral conversion (*Aparecida* 368–70) was now viewed in relation to "spiritual, pastoral, and institutional reforms" (*Aparecida* 367), thus taking a further step and considering it necessary to "abandon outdated structures that no longer favor the transmission of faith" (*Aparecida* 365). The Medellín document, issued by the *Second General Conference of Latin American Bishops* in 1968, had already sought ways to overcome the preconciliar Christendom model because it was "based on sacramentalization with little emphasis on prior evangelization" (*Medellín* 6.1).

Faithful to the Council's method and the spirit of Medellín, the Aparecida Conference sought "to listen to the signs of the times in which God manifests himself" (*Aparecida* 366). As a first step in achieving true reform, it proposed to shift "from a pastoral ministry of mere preservation to one that is decidedly missionary" (*Aparecida* 370). Having established the relation of this first step to the Church's missionary identity (*Aparecida* 347), the conference then proposed a model to be followed, namely, that of a "community of evangelized and missionary communities" (*Aparecida* 99) that joins together all the faithful as a collectively evangelizing subject.

In other words, what defines the identity of church members is their condition of being *missionary disciples*, a condition that flows from the equality of all the faithful in the dignity of baptism. In this new model, "pastoral conversion requires that the ecclesial communities be communities of *missionary disciples* assembled around Jesus Christ, Teacher, and Pastor. That condition gives rise to the attitudes of openness, dialogue, and availability that are needed to promote the coresponsibility and effective participation of *all the faithful* in the life of the Christian communities" (*Aparecida* 368). In this way, a deep correlation is established between pastoral conversion, the ecclesiological model, and ecclesial governance.

THE PATH OF PASTORAL CONVERSION

In adopting the ideal of pastoral conversion, Aparecida repositioned the model of Church communion within the *People of God* model, thus reaffirming a *synodal way of proceeding* in which "the laity must participate in *discernment, decision-taking, planning,* and *implementation*" (*Aparecida* 371). This text has been key in the current process of the reform of CELAM—the Latin American Council of Bishops.[11] Here are the emerging signs of a synodal-type ecclesiology—one that includes everyone in the processes of *discernment, decision-taking, planning,* and *implementation*—and that has its roots in its declaration that we are *the evangelizing People of God* (*Aparecida* 157). Therefore, "the vocation to missionary discipleship is a *summoning* to communion in the Church" (*Aparecida* 156) among the diverse subjects and levels that comprise the Church. In this context, the missionary discipleship ecclesiology of Aparecida that is essential for understanding Francis, carries the seed of a synodal Church. This is expressed extraordinarily in the declaration in which *Aparecida* describes the bishop in relation to the people of God:

> *Along with all the faithful and by virtue of baptism, we [bishops] are primarily disciples and members of the People of God.* Like all the baptized, and together with them, we want to follow Jesus, Teacher of life and truth, in the communion of the Church. (*Aparecida* 186)

By following the *path of pastoral conversion,* Latin American ecclesiology has sought to overcome the primacy that the 1985 Extraordinary Synod granted to the model of vertical communion; it orients us instead toward a fluid, horizontal communion, both *ad intra* (among all the baptized) and *ad extra* (with all humanity), in fidelity to the Council's call for a *communio ecclesiarum,* which has been key to the creation and existence of CELAM based on a model of the Church as a *Church of churches.*

Consequently, *the preconciliar ecclesial pyramid is inverted,* and this inversion obliges us to undertake an *organic reform* that not only reevaluates lifestyles and ways of relating, but also rethinks the dynamics and management of power in ecclesial structures in light of the ecclesiology of the people of God. For Francis, this ecclesiology, "the missionary discipleship which Aparecida proposed to the Churches of Latin America and the Caribbean is the journey which *God desires for the present 'today.'*"[12] This path opened by pastoral conversion will be deepened and will lead to the need for a *synodal reform.*

In the light of synodality, we can make progress in the reception of the Council in our own day, since synodality must become the structuring principle of a process of ecclesiogenesis that begins with pastoral conversion and involves the whole people of God in the processes of ecclesial *discernment, planning, decision-taking,* and *cogovernance.* The ecclesiological proposal of the current pontificate cannot be understood without this connection between the *pastoral* conversion and *synodal* conversion of the whole Church. The conjunction of the two concepts gives rise to a new definition of the Church's identity and mission and opens a new phase in the reception of Vatican II.

This new phase can be characterized by an ecclesiological shift that involves the beginning of a *transition* from a Western, monocultural Church, centered on Rome and the primacy, to a global and intercultural Church,[13] thus opening the way to recognizing the authority of the local churches (see *EG* 32). The series of Synods under Francis are an example of this transition, as a place of convergence and communion building among the local churches, and between local churches and the universal Church and the Bishop of Rome.

This shift has triggered a chain of ongoing processes of reform that directly affect lifestyles, discernment practices, and governance structures, such as those put into practice in the reform of the curia. In this new understanding, coresponsibility is no longer an auxiliary relationship, but an essential one, capable of granting and cosharing *power of jurisdiction* with those who do not have the *power of order*. This has already happened with the appointment of several laywomen and -men to high-level positions in the Vatican, formerly reserved only to bishops.[14]

3

Introducing Synodality

A NEW ECCLESIAL MODEL

In his speech at the Commemoration of the Fiftieth Anniversary of the Institution of the Synod of Bishops, Pope Francis not only defined the nature of the Church but also specified the direction in which Church reform should move:

> The path of synodality is the path that *God expects* of the Church of the third millennium. What the Lord asks of us is already contained, in a sense, in the word "synod," which means "walking together"—*laity, pastors, Bishop of Rome.*[1]

Here, the reference to the *third millennium* is key to the interpretation of synodality, because it represents the overcoming of a pyramidal and hierarchical institutional model and of a homogenizing way of carrying out evangelization. Both phenomena were born in the *second millennium* and implemented by the Gregorian Reforms and the Council of Trent. They are still present today in our lifestyles, our communicative dynamics, and our relationships, revealing a fissure in the reception of the Second Vatican Council. That is why, following Paul VI,[2] Francis wants to deepen the reform in light of "the spirit and the method" of the Council. That means, in the words of the International Theological Commission (ITC), that "although synodality is not explicitly found as a term or a concept in the teaching of Vatican II, it is fair to say that synodality is at the heart of the work of renewal the Council was encouraging."[3]

The ITC describes synodality as a "constitutive dimension of the whole Church" because it characterizes the Church's "specific way of living and working (*modus vivendi et operandi*)." We can define synodality even more precisely as an *ecclesial way of proceeding*, meaning that it is a *constituent*, processual reality rather than simply a particular practice of a functional and organizational nature. Synodality involves the constant review *of lifestyles* (spirit) and *discernment practices* (method) at all *levels* and *structures of government*. It is the application of the classical medieval principle according to which *what affects everyone must be discussed and approved by everyone (quod omnes tangit ab omnibus tractari et approbari debet).*[4]

Since synodality is a *constitutive* and *constituent* dimension of ecclesiality, it cannot be identified with a specific event, nor can it be reduced to a method. Synodality is much more than the classical institutional forms—such as councils, synods, or conferences—through which it has traditionally been practiced.[5] Neither is synodality a new ecclesial model. Rather, it is what makes a new model possible by setting in motion a process of constant ecclesiogenesis that generates an ecclesial way of proceeding.[6] Synodality engenders a structuring, transversal spirit of ecclesiality that results in an ecclesiology. It is a new *mark*, a novel ecclesial hermeneutics that reconfigures the identities and relationships among all ecclesial subjects, as well as the organization and institutional model articulated by the structures of the Church. In Zamnon's words, "Synodality is the form in which the recognition of multiple subjectivities can take place, all of them necessary, albeit in different ways, for the fulfillment of the Church's mission."[7]

Bernard Franck argues that "the essence of synodality is a spirit rather than a principle"[8] because it stresses and reconfigures the *relationships and processes* among subjects to achieve "unity in plurality," the "whole in the parts." By virtue of synodality, the *sensus ecclesiae*, the whole ecclesial reality, is activated, and the normativity of each existing ecclesial *subjectivity* is recognized. According to Franck, this is achieved through participatory dynamics such as "reciprocal listening, exchange and communication, sharing and solidarity, the desire to reach a consensus and common conviction. This requires the willingness to collaborate and to cooperate, to accept and to welcome, to give and to receive. This supposes relationships steeped in respect and charity, humility and poverty. This is the 'synodal' spirit."[9]

AN ECCLESIAL WAY OF PROCEEDING

Francis boldly affirms that "a synodal Church is a *Church that listens*, because it is aware that listening 'is more than hearing.' It is a reciprocal listening in which everyone—faithful people, episcopal college, Bishop of Rome—has something to learn, each one listening to the others; and all listening to the Holy Spirit, the 'Spirit of truth' (John 14:17), in order to know what he 'is saying to the Churches' (Rev 2:7)."[10] To implement this new way of proceeding,

all are invited to listen to one another, to discern pastoral decisions and implement them together, with all doing their part. It is a matter of discerning what the Spirit of Christ is saying to the Church, which he is building *in this place*. For the Spirit "speaks" through diverse *mediations*, such as our hearing the Gospel, the silence of prayer, the reviewing of life and events in the light of faith, the confrontation of differing viewpoints, etc.[11]

Therefore, it is not a listening only through traditional mediations—Gospel, prayer, and so on—but also, and above all, through the confrontation of different viewpoints, face-to-face, in an ambience and with a method of communal discernment. This method allows everyone to freely express their points of view with an attitude of openness to learning and relearning new ways of seeing and valuing issues in life and in the Church. In this way, what is heard and discerned from the people should then find ecclesial channels and structures—or, as Francis said, "concrete mediations"—that link it to magisterial decisions. A new mentality implies developing a more complete understanding of the theology of the *sensus fidelium* and its implications for ecclesial decisions at all levels.

We can speak of the need to develop a *synodal style* that involves listening, discernment, dialogue, and a cosharing of the exercise of power based on consensus-building practices. This implies creating a relational dynamic, a human environment, and accountable practices. Without these capacities, it is impossible to develop the reform processes that *Medellín* says are necessary to guarantee "constant change of structures, transformation of attitudes, and conversion of hearts" (*Medellín, Paz* 14). What is novel in the vision of Francis is not synodality, itself; it is his conviction that synodality can be made a reality only through *pastoral conversion*,[12] as we have previously explained. This was made clear by Pope Francis when he stated,

> Reform of the Curia comes about not simply with a change of persons—which undoubtedly happens and will continue to happen—but with *the conversion of persons*. In reality, "permanent formation" is not enough; what is necessary, above all, is "permanent conversion and purification." *Without a "change of mentality" a dutiful effort will be useless.*[13]

True reform involves the conversion of both clericalized mentalities and clericalized structures, and all that that implies, as described above. We can therefore state that synodality is above all an *ecclesial way of proceeding* that starts from what is ambient and not necessarily thematic or consciously thematized since it implies a building up of the base of the pyramid. From that base, synodality will promote pastoral conversion grounded in relations of horizontal communion that spiral upward toward the hierarchy but are always driven by processes of convergence that link all subjects. All this requires a reform of mentalities that will pave the way for the development of synodal attitudes such as listening, discernment, and dialogue.

Without this change of mentality, none of the institutional processes of reform required in this new millennium will come about. This is a decisive factor in any synodal process, but we cannot neglect the warning of Alphonse Borras:

> Besides the informal synodality resulting from the mutual listening and partnership of the baptized in mission, there is a more formal synodality practiced in more or less formalized ways and at different levels of

institutionalization. Synodal practices are not limited either to the synodal institutions that exist at any given time in the history of the Church or to the procedures that they provide or sanction. It is the case, though, that *synodality can hardly exist without institutional places or procedures for implementation.*[14]

Therefore, while it is true that synodality involves listening to one another as *we walk along,* we must recognize that synodality takes place only when we *gather and discern together* so as to activate modalities and processes of decision-making and decision-taking that involve the participation of the whole and the parts (*LG* 13). Regarding the necessary modalities and processes, a challenging case is presented by the discernment practices and the type of votes in a synodal assembly.

The problem lies not only in determining the deliberative vote of the majority, or the principle of the *maior pars,* but also in discerning the minority vote, be it consultative or deliberative, representing the *sanior pars.* The subject throughout the whole synodal process must always be *the totality of the faithful,*[15] which expresses itself through forms, procedures, and structures of the community—rather than of merely particular groups—to achieve a consensus that is binding for all. But *ecclesial consensus* can be created only within the setting of a fraternal spirit that encourages the participation and free interaction of all.[16] Otherwise, the results will be simply formal, and not necessarily representative of the whole people of God.

Therefore, the challenge is to create and institutionalize more modalities and mechanisms of *effective* and inclusive participation, capable of creating the *link* between "one, some, and all." In *Evangelii Gaudium,* Francis emphasizes the important role played by the bishop in this process:

In his mission of fostering a dynamic, open and missionary communion, he will have to encourage and develop the means of participation proposed in the Code of Canon Law, as well as other forms of pastoral dialogue, out of a desire to listen to everyone and not simply to those who would tell him what he would like to hear. Yet the principal aim of these participatory processes should not be ecclesiastical organization but rather the missionary aspiration of reaching everyone. (*EG* 31)

4

Synodality and Decision-Making

THE WHOLE COMMUNITY

F rancis's deepening of the synodal path advances our reflection on the ways in which all the faithful participate and to what extent they are incorporated in decision-making, as well as in the ministerial dimension of the Church. Remember, too, the call made by *Aparecida*, namely, that all the faithful must participate in discernment, decision-taking, planning, and implementation (*Aparecida* 371). In defining a *synodal Church*, the International Theological Commission follows this principle and provides us with two basic interpretive keys:

(a) "In the synodal Church *the whole community*, in the free and rich diversity of its members, is called together to pray, listen, analyze, dialogue, discern and offer advice *on taking pastoral decisions* which correspond as closely as possible to God's will."[1]

(b) "A synodal Church is a *Church of participation and co-responsibility.* In exercising synodality, it is called to allow for *the participation of all, according to each one's calling,* with the authority conferred by Christ on the College of Bishops headed by the Pope. Participation is based on the fact that all the faithful are qualified and are called to serve one another through the gifts they have all received from the Holy Spirit."[2]

Ultimately, what is at stake is the very model of Church that we can adopt. The ecclesiological model is decisive for conceiving the subjects and their modalities of participation, as well as for determining the role of ordained ministers in the decision-making and decision-taking processes. If the Church is understood as being basically a *missionary disciple,* then "the totality of the People of God is the subject" of all the processes that must be discerned so that the Church can fulfill its mission. As already stated, all the activities are oriented so that the "whole community *makes pastoral decisions."*

This supposes that if "synodality is the form that allows for the recognition of multiple subjectivities, all of which are necessary to fulfill the Church's mission, though in different ways,"[3] then no one can be excluded from the call to participate. Such participation necessarily involves, however, the recovery of a model of ministerial Church that can "activate in *synodal synergy* the *ministries and charisms*"[4] that are present in ecclesial life for discerning its mission today. A ministerial Church bases its relationships on charisms and gifts rather than on order and power. Hence, the processes for elaborating and making decisions should be conceived of in terms of horizontality and circularity.

Consequently, synodality cannot be limited to the convening of events, such as episcopal conferences or the celebration of synods. Synods are just one form of synodal event and structure. What is called for is the *synodalization* of the whole Church because that is the preeminently *ecclesial way of proceeding*, and as such, it is a *transversal lynchpin* that, growing out of a fraternal ambience (*affectus*), gradually produces the bond that translates into decisions, which must then be institutionally and canonically formalized (*effectus*). Synodality, therefore, requires "implementation in the local Church and on every level of the circular relationship linking pastoral ministry, lay participation and coresponsibility, and the impulses coming from charismatic gifts, according to the dynamic circularity among 'one,' 'some,' and 'all.'"[5] When this relationship exists, it presupposes that the specific function of the ordained ministry of bishops, priests, and deacons will be well coordinated with the community in which they live and serve.

This is made possible, according to Gilles Routhier, through *dialogue*, which is the mechanism that gives form to the whole synodal process through a series of actions or practices such as *expressing opinions, listening,* and *taking counsel,*[6] and furthermore, by proceeding in this way, the whole community will be represented in the decision made by the authority. We can speak, then, of a *synodal way of proceeding* characterized by several steps that include the following:

(a) *Taking counsel in the Church,* which means *seeing* the reality, gathering data, and listening to diverse opinions

(b) *Judging* and evaluating what is gathered in this process

(c) Applying what is judged good to the mission of the Church—in other words, *acting*

(d) And all this followed by permanent evaluations and accountable procedures

When we use this method, it obliges us to implement dynamics that, Routhier claims,

> favor complete dissemination of information, encourage the search for and serene expression of various points of view, support study that helps ideas mature, frame the interchange and deliberation that lead to decision-making, promote feedback in order to understand better the directions taken, etc. These procedures encourage meetings, exchanges, and dialogues, thus establishing ongoing relationships and interactions among persons.[7]

THE SYNODAL PROCESS OF DECISION-MAKING

Regarding the modalities of participation and the creation of bonds, "it is necessary to distinguish between the process of decision-making through a joint exercise of discernment, consultation, and co-operation, and the decision-taking that is within the competence of the Bishop, the guarantor of apostolicity and Catholicity. Working things out is a synodal task; decision is a ministerial responsibility."[8] Importantly, these two moments of the process are not to be considered as separate but as mutually reinforcing. That is why the International Theological Commission speaks of the circularity that integrates *sensus fidei, discernment,* and *authority* by virtue of the baptismal dignity and coresponsibility of all. If this circularity is effective, then the *decision-making* process will not be very different from the process that precedes the final decision that is taken.

> The *entire* People of God is challenged by its fundamentally synodal calling. The *circularity* of the *sensus fidei* with which all the faithful are endowed, the *discernment* carried out at the various levels on which synodality works, and the *authority* of those who exercise the pastoral ministry of unity and governance, all demonstrate the dynamic of synodality. This circularity promotes the baptismal dignity and co-responsibility of all, [and it] makes the most of the presence in the People of God of charisms dispensed by the Holy Spirit.[9]

The challenge, then, is to ensure that the modalities of participation with which this *circularity* functions can *incorporate and involve subjects* who, until now, have been absent or considered only auxiliary, and to *produce binding decisions*. For this to happen, it is necessary to recognize the normative and reciprocal character of the vocation of every ecclesial subject in relation to the subject's interaction with the rest. Once again, the problem we are facing is not merely methodological and functional; it is the problem of an ecclesiological model.

The Council reminds us that the Word of God has been entrusted to "the entire People of God united with their shepherds" (*Dei Verbum* 10) and that, because of this *union*, which is normative, they must "form one single consensus" (*fidelium conspiratio*). That is why the International Theological Commission maintains that this *circularity* and the decisions arising from this circularity are binding on all and that its aim is *to reach agreement "on discerning the truth and on the missionary path to take."* Such agreement translates into decision, but not the reverse. The Commission states,

> Synodality as an essential dimension of the Church is expressed on the level of the universal Church in the *dynamic circularity* of the *consensus fidelium*, episcopal collegiality and the primacy of the Bishop of Rome. On this basis, the Church is asked from time to time to respond—in fidelity to the *depositum fidei* and in creative openness to the voice of the Spirit—to particular circumstances and challenges; she is called to *set in motion a process of listening to all the subjects who together form the People of God in order to agree in discerning the truth and on the missionary path to take.*[10]

The mechanisms and procedures of *consultation* cannot be the only factors, or even the most important factors, for arriving at decisions in a synodal process, and neither can the views of isolated individuals. Rather, as we have insisted, *dialogue* and *communal discernment* are the essential elements in *preparing to make decisions* based on the practices of convergence and consensus building. The binding force is found in this aspect of the *decision-making* process. Indeed, this element is what makes the process authentically synodal: when it is lacking, *decision-taking* can easily revert to the pyramidal ecclesial model that needs to be overcome.

A concrete example of this can be found in the relationship between the consultative vote and the deliberative vote. The consultative vote is a *constituent* part of the process that gives rise to the *consensus fidelium*; it represents the reciprocal relationship among laity, priests, and bishops without which no consensus could be formulated. In this sense, it must be binding. In other words, the deliberative vote of the bishops must be made *within* the people of God, because it is the decisive testimony and final articulation of the process that begins with the consultative vote of all the faithful and in interaction with them. Thus, the deliberative vote must express the *sentire cum ecclesia* and not simply the views of the hierarchy, as if they could subsist outside the *communio fidelium*.[11] For this reason, the decision-taking of the *many* (episcopal collegiality) and the *one* (primacy) cannot be separated from the *decision-making* of *all* (the faithful, who include the bishops and the pope).

Certainly, the consultation procedures are indispensable for making a more considered judgment about what should be discussed, but the *participation of all in the mission* of the Church goes far beyond that. The reason why all must participate, as we have explained, is that the *discernment, decision-taking, planning,* and *implementation* (*Aparecida* 371) required for this mission are, *in conscience*, the responsibility of all and not just a few, and as such they must find adequate modalities and structures.[12] The challenge today is clear: the reform of mentalities must be linked to the reform of structures; what is more, a true *synodalization* of the whole Church can be carried out only in conjunction with an organic revision of the Code of Canon Law. It is useful here to recall the words of Cardinal Suenens when evaluating the Council:

> The future of the new canon law will depend on how the principle of subsidiarity is applied .... The principle was reaffirmed at the first Synod of Bishops and has been considered theoretically solid. The success of the new code will depend on the extent to which it is inspired by the spirit of Vatican II and translates into

legislation the theology of the Church we evoked at the start.[13]

We must recognize, then, that such a task always poses the question of the alignment of the Council's ecclesiology and the Code of Canon Law and that needs, therefore, to bring together theologians and canon lawyers. Even so, after the Council, theologians were more preoccupied with studying the new ecclesiology and much less with its implications for creating new structures. Similarly, canon lawyers centered their reflection more on the theological foundations of the new Code, and less on how the new ecclesiology would demand a nonclericalist institutional model of the Church based on the theological-structural implications of the normative character of chapter 2 of *Lumen Gentium* (On the People of God), as proposed by the Council fathers.

We conclude this section by agreeing with the challenge posed by Severino Dianich regarding the need of a reform of the current Code in relation to synodality:

> The problem is that of the consequences to be drawn on the level of regulations, so that the subject of the fundamental activity of the Church, Evangelization, is also a determining subject for various components of the internal life of the community. The current normativity, between the attribution to all the faithful of the task of evangelization—the principal source of the very existence of the Church—and their call to an active participation in the Eucharistic liturgy—which is the culmination of the life of the Church (*SC* 14)—does not give the lay faithful any specific role capable of determining the life of the community....The [lay] faithful do not have any instance in which, by expressing their

own deliberative vote, something could be collegially decided.[14]

Part of the problem is that the reform of the 1917 Code was concluded in 1983, in a phase of the reception of the Council that had not fully received the model of Church as people of God walking in communion, a Church of churches. Such a reception had yet to be fully realized. Synodality, as a deepening and advancement of the Council's ecclesiology, and as a new ecclesial hermeneutic, offers a way to do that: its scope should be the *synodalization* of the whole Church.

PART II

SYNODALITY AND THE PEOPLE OF GOD

5

The People of God as All the Faithful

RECOVERING THE NORMATIVE CHARACTER OF THE PEOPLE OF GOD

In 2013, we entered a new phase of conciliar reception that recovered the Church as *the people of God*—the central hermeneutical criterion and normative character of the Second Vatican Council's ecclesiology. In an interview with Antonio Spadaro in the first year of his pontificate, Francis spoke about "the Church as people of God, pastors and people together. The Church is the totality of the people of God."[1] This definition echoes the words of Cardinal Suenens, architect of *Lumen Gentium*, who emphasized the importance of this perspective when he stated,

> If we were to be asked what we consider to be that seed
> of life deriving from the council which is most fruitful
> in pastoral consequences, we would answer without
> any hesitation: it is the rediscovery of *the people of God*

as a whole, as a single reality; and then by way of consequence, the coresponsibility thus implied for every
member of the church.[2]

The cardinal's words contain two keys of interpretation: (1)
the people of God understood as a *totality*; and (2) the principle
of *coresponsibility* as the criterion for defining the relationships
among the different ecclesial subjects based on their respective
identities. The mid-1980s, however, saw the reception of the
Council enter a new phase, one marked by a shift in interpreting
its ecclesiology. The new interpretation gave priority to the category of hierarchical communion and subordinated the "sense of
the faithful" (*sensus fidelium*) to the magisterium. This change was
institutionalized in 1985 in the *Final Report* of the Extraordinary
Synod of Bishops, although it was already anticipated in the 1984
instruction of the Congregation for the Doctrine of the Faith,
Libertatis Nuntius, as well as in the 1985 document of the International Theological Commission, *Selected Themes in Ecclesiology*.

A change of orientation in the theological literature attests
to this shift. Arguments were put forward about the meaning
of unity, but this was understood as a type of uniformity based
on an overvaluation of the *communio hierarchica*, as if this could
somehow be nonbinding with respect to the *communio fidelium*.
The consequence was that the papacy and the episcopacy began
to be understood as distinct subjects in relation to the people of
God. There was a regression to a pyramidal conception, one that
understood the diverse modes of participation in the Church
as deriving formally from the *communio hierarchica*, and consequently discarded the theology of the *sensus omnium fidelium*.
This resulted in a notion of lay responsibility as an ancillary exercise and in the juxtaposition, still not fully resolved, between
episcopal collegiality and the primacy.

The People of God as All the Faithful

In line with Pope Paul VI, Francis goes back to the Council and states that "the Church, as the agent of evangelization, is more than an organic and hierarchical institution….She exists concretely in history as a people of pilgrims and evangelizers, transcending any institutional expression" (*EG* 111). In continuity with *Lumen Gentium* (*EG* 17), Francis affirms that "being Church means being God's people" (*EG* 114): "The People of God is incarnate in the peoples of the earth, each of which has its own culture" (*EG* 115). The recovery of this notion allows for a better understanding of the identities and relationships among the different ecclesial subjects, which are seen in light of the hermeneutical circularity of all the subjectivities and therefore of the Church itself as a collective organic subject that constitutes an *ecclesial we*.[3]

Each person is recognized as *one of the faithful* who, by reason of baptism, is made partaker of the *tria munera Christi*, in equality of conditions through the common priesthood. This is not a new or different way of understanding the Church; it simply highlights the centrality of the people of God in the Council's ecclesiological architecture, which was the intention of *Lumen Gentium*. In 1965, Congar explained,

> In the schema *De Ecclesia* the sequence might have been: the Mystery of the Church, Hierarchy, the People of God in general. This would have meant a failure to honor the third aim expressed above: to discuss what affects the quality that is shared by all the members of the Church, before examining how they are differentiated by their function or state of life. This would also have suggested the idea that the hierarchical organization represents the first value in the Church, that is, the distribution of members according to an order

of superiority or subordination. But the sequence adopted was: Mystery of the Church, People of God, Hierarchy. Thus, the highest value was given to the quality of disciple, the dignity attached to Christian existence as such or the reality of an ontology of grace, and then, to the interior of this reality, a hierarchical structure of social organization.[4]

This change of categories is not simply a response or an adaptation of the Church to modern times. As we have noted, it follows the intention of Paul VI in revealing a *complete definition* not only of the Church's identity and mission but also of its form and organization. Faithful to his vision, Francis has taken the first steps to realign chapters 2 and 3 of *Lumen Gentium*, making it clear that both papal primacy and collegiality require reform, that ordained ministry needs to be reconfigured in order to address the real issues on how power and authority are exercised and by whom in the Church; their raison d'être and their exercise must be understood in the context of the people of God and in light of the relational framework provided by synodality.

Such a framework understands hierarchy in terms of its transitory, historical character, rather than as an ontological, eschatological, or self-referential reality. Bishop De Smedt had already expressed this during the conciliar debates: "We must be careful when speaking about the Church so as not to fall into a certain hierarchism, clericalism, and bishopolatry or papolatry. *What comes first is the People of God.*"[5] As the International Theological Commission explains,

The sequence—the Mystery of the Church (chapter 1), the People of God (chapter 2), the Hierarchical Constitution of the Church (chapter 3)—stresses that the ecclesiastical hierarchy is at the service of the People of God in order that the Church may carry out her mission in conformity with God's plan of salvation, in the logic of the priority of the whole over its parts and of the end over the means.[6]

It is because of this hermeneutical ecclesiological framework that we can talk about synodality. Otherwise, it will be very difficult, if not impossible, to clear the hurdles of clericalized ecclesial culture and excessively priest-centered ministries.[7] A great deal of the problem we face today when talking about synodality has to do with an incomplete or selective reception of the ecclesiology of the texts and the spirit of the Council, understood as an event and a Constitutional Text of the Universal Church. Because of these obstacles, a large part of the hierarchy has lost "direct contact with the People of God" and so exercises its power in isolation and from above.[8]

In an address to the Chilean bishops regarding one of the major ongoing ecclesial crises in the world, Francis acknowledged the normative character of the people of God for the conversion of the Church and its "perennial reform" (*UR* 6): "In this faithful and silent people lies the immune system of the Church" (*Private Letter to the Bishops of Chile*). The pontiff also invited "all the diocesan organizations—whatever their area—to seek out consciously and lucidly spaces for communion and participation *so that the Anointing of the People of God finds concrete ways to make itself manifest*"[9] because "renewal in the ecclesial hierarchy does not by itself produce the transformation toward which the Holy Spirit impels us."[10]

This text calls not only for a change in mentalities on the part of the hierarchy but also for the creation of concrete mediations of a structural nature that allow all members of the people of

God, and not just a few, to participate in the ecclesiastical institution. All this change requires new relational and communicational dynamics that acknowledge and implement the reciprocal and binding character that must exist between the *hierarchical communion* and *communio fidelium*, for both together constitute the *universitas fidelium*. The hermeneutics of the conciliar expression, *Christifideles*, opens a new path in the formulas of communication and participation among the ecclesial subjects that make up the people of God, and it allows us to rethink the definition of their identities within the framework of an ecclesial missionary "we."

WE ARE ALL *CHRISTIFIDELES*

During the conciliar discussions, Bishop Joseph De Smedt effected a break with the pyramidal model, a model that favored the parts over the whole by conceiving the hierarchy as a separate subject, distinct from the rest of the people of God. His vision involved overcoming mentalities and structures inspired by the triumphalism, juridicism, and clericalism that had characterized the life and mission of the Church for almost a millennium. During his intervention, he described the needed shift quite boldly:

> You are familiar with the pyramid: pope, bishops, priests, each of them responsible; they teach, sanctify, and rule with due authority. Then, at the base, the Christian people, who are more than anything receptive, in accordance with the place they seem to occupy in the Church....[In contrast,] *in the People of God, we are all united with one another, and we have the same fundamental laws and duties.* We all participate in the royal priesthood of the People of God. The Pope is

one of the faithful; bishops, priests, laity, religious, *we are all [the] faithful* ... .We must be careful when speaking about the Church [therefore] so as not to fall into hierarchicalism, clericalism, and bishopolatry or papolatry. *What comes first is the People of God.*[11]

For the bishop of Bruges, the novelty was not to be found in rearranging the subjects in a new, inverted pyramid; it was not a matter of changing places, positioning the people of God above and the hierarchy below. Such an inversion would change order between them, but they would continue to be seen as separate ecclesial subjects.

The path toward novelty would become possible through a new hermeneutic of dynamic relations and communications among all the members of the ecclesial body; this new logic would reclassify ecclesial identities and their respective participation in the Church's mission. For De Smedt, the order of the proposed sequence—first, the people of God (all), then the bishops (some), and finally the Bishop of Rome (one)—was an effort to move beyond the previous vision of three distinct ecclesial subjects (pope, bishops, and people of God) by integrating the bishops and the pope into the *totality of the people of God* as part of the *faithful*, or *Christifideles*.

The *mens* of the conciliar texts found its inspiration in this integrating hermeneutic that incorporates all ecclesial subjects (including the episcopal college and successor of Peter) into the *totality* of all the faithful, whose continual and reciprocal interaction progressively constitutes them as the people of God. Insofar as it encompasses the totality of the faithful in their permanent relationships and communicational dynamics, the people of God is fundamentally the only active subject of the whole of the Church's action and mission.

Bishop De Smedt pointed out cogently that the people of God "are all united with one another, and we have the same fundamental laws and duties. We all participate in the royal priesthood of the people of God. The Pope is one of the faithful; bishops, priests, laity, religious, *we are all [the] faithful*."[12] Similarly, the Council had reaffirmed that "everything that has been said concerning the people of God is intended for laity, religious, and clergy alike" (*LG* 30). The *principle of totality* assumes that ecclesial life is defined by the relational, by what is reciprocal and complementary, by an ecclesial style and way of proceeding that prioritizes the "common work [and] participation of all according to the diversity and originality of their gifts and services."[13] All this is based on the common condition that permits the exercise of the *tria munera*—the functions of teaching, sanctifying, and governing—in the context of the reciprocal interaction that must take place among all ecclesial subjects.

The Council used the expression *Christifideles* to describe the common condition that defines the various ecclesial identities; it is a term that is neither univocal nor equivocal in defining what is proper to each subject with respect to the others. The term *faithful* seeks to stress the multifaceted and coresponsible nature of the relationships *among all* the members[14] within the people of God—bishops, priests, lay, and religious. As *Lumen Gentium* emphasizes, "Every member is at the service of the other members…[so that] the pastors and the other faithful are bound to each other *by a mutual need*" (*LG* 32). All the members together constitute a totality that is realized through a shared dynamic as the people of God, a people characterized by relations of reciprocal and complementary interactions, according to which each member, *suo modo et pro sua parte* ("in their own way and their own part"; *LG* 31), is defined *in relation to* the others and completes the others.

We can speak, therefore, of the ecclesial process of building an organic totality, an ecclesial "we," that goes beyond the clerical, *hierarchological* model of the Church as an unequal society. As Cardinal Suenens explained, "In the People of God, the functions, tasks, ministries, states of life, and charisms are linked *organically* in a multifaceted network of structural links and vital relationships (*LG* 13)."[15]

The Council's ecclesiological shift is best expressed in *Lumen Gentium* (no. 12), which speaks of the relational logic and reciprocal interaction among the various ecclesial subjects. This is perhaps one of the texts that have found less receptivity in the postconciliar literature. The reason is that the novelty is not in the definition of ecclesial identities per se; it is rather in the logic with which the identities are interpreted and in the consequences of such logic for the reform of the entire ecclesial organization. Thus, the category of people of God, as the totality of the faithful in mutual reciprocity, becomes a hermeneutical principle; its ontological normativity defines the roles and functions of each *Christifidelis* in a constitutive, processual manner.

The essential qualification is the *baptism* that makes us all coresponsible members with equal dignity in the mission. We are, therefore, all part of the base, as persons of faith who are becoming the people of God through our daily horizontal relationships. A couple of years after the Council, Cardinal Suenens described this process:

> The Church, viewed in terms of baptism rather than hierarchy, appeared from the start as a sacramental and mystical reality before also being a juridical society. *It rests on its base, the people of God, instead of on its point, the hierarchy.* The pyramid of our manuals had been *inverted*: a Roman prelate could write that it was

a true Copernican revolution. For this very reason, the bishop…must again *become situated in the people of God* entrusted to him: he must be ever closer to his clergy and his faithful, living in the same conditions as they, even in terms of clothing.[16]

It was not just a question of starting out from the base, as if the change could be reduced to a simple reshuffling of places in a new pyramid; rather, the aim was above all *to include all the ecclesial subjects in that peripheral base as a meeting point from which they would move toward the center.* The ecclesiological shift intended a *new ecclesial way of proceeding* that grants primacy to two fundamental principles: (a) "the whole over the parts," highlighting baptismal dignity and the participation of all equally in the common priesthood;[17] and (b) "from the periphery to the center," calling for the horizontal exercise of the *sensus omnium fidelium*, whereby the totality of the people of God, the episcopal college, and the successor of Peter are all integrated and articulated, but in that specific order; namely, *the people of God (all)*, then *the bishops (some)*, and finally, *the Bishop of Rome (one)*.

It is in this context that Francis states that "the pope is not, by himself, above the Church; rather, he is within it as *one baptized among the baptized*, and he is within the episcopal college as *one bishop among bishops*."[18] This is what he had envisioned in 2013 as an essential part of the reform: the "conversion of the papacy" as a step toward the decentralization that the Church needs (*EG* 32). The principle of hierarchical ministry is to be understood in terms of the search for unity and consensus, and not as a vertical chain of command; we should therefore understand the exercise of collegiality in a double sense: affective (*collegialitas affectiva*) and effective (*collegialitas effectiva*).

The People of God as All the Faithful

The objective of inverting the pyramid is not to improve collegial practice, by seeking a better balance between the episcopal college and the exercise of papal primacy, nor is it merely a redistribution of ecclesial coresponsibility. The inversion of the pyramid entails adopting an ecclesial style, a new institutional model and a way of proceeding that translate into a search for appropriate mechanisms, spaces, and modes for carrying out the "common work" with "the participation of all according to the diversity and originality of gifts and services."[19] Francis explains it well:

> In virtue of their baptism, all the members of the People of God have become missionary disciples (cf. Matt 28:19). All the baptized, whatever their position in the Church or their level of instruction in the faith, are agents of evangelization, and it would be insufficient to envisage a plan of evangelization to be carried out by professionals while the rest of the faithful would simply be passive recipients. (*EG* 120)

And again, Francis follows the Council when he states,

> In this Church, as an *inverted pyramid*, the top is below the base. That is why those who exercise authority are called "ministers": according to the original meaning of the word, they are the least of all. Each Bishop serving the People of God becomes, for the portion of the flock entrusted to him, a *vicarius Christi*, a vicar of Jesus, who at the Last Supper stooped down to wash the apostles' feet (cf. John 13:1–15). By the same logic, the Successor of Peter is himself the *servus servorum Dei*.[20]

Even though the image of an inverted pyramid remains incomplete for the reforms that are needed today, we cannot forget that it refers to a radical change of the ecclesiological model and not simply to its renewal. The constitution *Pastor Aeternus* of Vatican I (1869–70) built its ecclesiology on the image of a *perfect society*; by asserting papal infallibility, it elevated the centrality of the pope's primacy over the episcopal college and the laity, so that the Church's juridical aspect was stressed over its reality as communion. According to this schema, the magisterium resided fully in the pope and only by participation in the episcopal college. The dominant model, that of a pyramid, was the result of the Gregorian Reforms that sharply distinguished the *ecclesia docens*—the only active subject, holding the power to interpret and to teach—from the *ecclesia discens*—the passive subject that listens and obeys. This model was well summarized in the *Decree of Gratian*, which distinguished two classes of persons by reason of their power: the clergy and the laity—those who preside and the subjects who obey.[21]

In fidelity to the spirit and the texts of the Council, we note that the hierarchy does not exhaust the reality of Church, nor can the Church, in its identity and mission, be thought of as a sacred subject that is distinct or separated from the people of God. If the people of God, both in its totality and in its interaction, is the only active subject of the Church's mission, the hierarchy can neither act nor claim an identity outside the people of God. There is no "rest" of the faithful identifiable with the laity and having only the function of assisting the hierarchical ministry. Once again, we are mindful of the wise words of the bishop of Bruges, who throws light on the *mens* of conciliar texts:

> The word *faithful* designates all those who have received the dignity of being members of the church by reason

of baptism. Therefore, the *faithful* are not only the laity but also the religious, the priests, the bishops, and the Pope. *Faithful* and *laity* are not interchangeable terms. When we find a mention of the *People of God*, it refers to the community made up of all the baptized, that is, of *all the faithful*.[22]

In this interpretation of the Council, the hierarchy is called to express not the views of the bishops, but the *sensus ecclesiae totius populi*. The implications of this ecclesiological shift continue to resonate today, pointing to a new way of being Church in which the ordained ministry's identity and mission are reconceived in the light of *Lumen Gentium*, chapter 2 ("On the People of God"). We can identify here one of the constitutive elements of the current phase of the Council's reception,[23] which, since 2013, has rescued this normativity.

This vision did not prosper only in Europe, nor was it deduced exclusively from a theological theory. It arose also in Latin America as the result of the practice of *lived contextual ecclesiality* experienced in a missionary context. This can be appreciated in the *vota* or proposals requested by Cardinal Tardini in the consultation process that started after John XXIII called for a new Ecumenical Council in 1959. Among the reflections of Bishop Leonidas Proaño from Ecuador, we find this: *the Church is all of us, the faithful*. Proaño seemed to be anticipating the conciliar model of the Church as people of God when he stated, "*Ecclesia non est unus Pontifex. Non est Pontifex cum Hierarchico Ordine: Ecclesia sumus omnes fideles in Christo baptizati. Omnes homines, etiam non baptizati, sunt Christi membra* in potentia."[24] Thus, if the Church is *all the faithful*, all ecclesial subjects have a missionary responsibility by reason of their baptism.

6

Reciprocity and Respectivity

THE PRIESTHOOD OF THE FAITHFUL AND THE ORDAINED MINISTRY

During the drafting of *Lumen Gentium* emerged the logic of reciprocity and respectivity, a logic that helps to explain the shift that the document's vision represented with respect to the preconciliar ecclesiology. The first outline of the *Constitution* stated,

> One priesthood does not exclude the other; on the contrary, both the ministerial priesthood and the universal priesthood, which differ in essence and not only in degree, originate, each in its own way, from the priesthood of Christ and are mutually ordained one to the other.[1]

The *textus prior* enunciated this same idea.[2] Both texts used the word "degree," to which we referred previously, to avoid any equivocity between the two types of priesthood. It was not a term indicating the superiority of one with respect to the other, but a term expressing diversity in unity. This reading was confirmed when the doctrinal commission decided to use the word "common"[3] instead of "universal," thereby indicating that the priesthood proper to all the baptized is analogous—neither the same nor completely different—to the ordained ministry of a few.[4] The analogy is that these priesthoods participate in the same unique priesthood of Christ, but in different ways.

The priesthood of the faithful highlights the personal dedication of the faithful's own existence, whereas the ministerial priesthood makes a corporate offering on behalf of all in the eucharistic celebration, acting as a symbol of communion and a prolongation of Christ's mission (cf. *Presbyterorum Ordinis* [*PO*] 12). Although both priesthoods are founded on the sacrament of baptism and participate in the unique priesthood of Christ (*LG* 62), the hierarchical priesthood operates specifically through the sacrament of orders, which bestows on it a ministerial function, namely, serving the community and presiding over the assembly by *acting in persona Christi* (*SC* 33; *PO* 2). This conception supersedes the Tridentine interpretation of the *alter Christus* based on the *potestas ordinis*.

The theology of the common priesthood has not been easily received in the Church because it requires us to recognize that the text and the spirit of the Council placed the ordained ministry within the people of God. The key element, as noted earlier, is the normative character of the sequence proposed by Cardinal Suenens, which placed chapter 2 ("On the People of God") of *Lumen Gentium* before chapter 3 ("On the Hierarchical Structure of the Church")[5] and made the former the lynchpin for defining the foundational identity of all ecclesial subjects in a dynamic of reciprocity and respectivity. This dynamic effectively dismantles the concentration of power, the separation of clergy and laity, and the hierarchy's authority by reason of ordination.

In this context, the Council situated the hierarchy within the organic whole of believers, declaring that "the pastors must be at the service of the other faithful" (*LG* 32). The ministerial priesthood, in its respectivity, is only one form of life by means of which some *Christifideles* realize their Christian vocation (*LG* 40–41).[6] This conciliar hermeneutic can be appreciated in the two interpretive sequences offered by *Lumen Gentium* and *Presbyterorum Ordinis*.

The sequence found in *Presbyterorum Ordinis* is, first, "*all the faithful* are made a holy and royal priesthood"; second, "*some* are ministers by sacramental order"; and third, "the ministers act in collaboration with the episcopal order" (*PO* 2). The sequence found in *Lumen Gentium* provides criteria for understanding the specific functions of the ministerial priesthood: first, the evangelizing function or proclamation of the Word, which is common to all the faithful, or *Christifideles*; second, the sacramental function; and third, the governing function (*LG* 25–28). The order of each sequence is normative for determining the identity of the hierarchical ministry within the people of God. What defines the primacy of that identity is the phrase "*primum habent officium Evangelium Dei omnibus evangelizandi*," that is, the "principal" function is announcing the "Word" (*PO* 4). Therefore, the priesthood exists not as a power over the Eucharist, as Trent maintained, but to serve the *evangelizing mission* for which all the faithful are equally coresponsible.

The normativity of the two sequences allows us to reaffirm what Bishop De Smedt asserted with great boldness: "Hierarchical power is only transitory....What is permanent is the people of God; what is transient is hierarchical service,"[7] which is conditioned by time and space (*pertinet ad statum viae*). The Church, therefore, is defined and constituted by what is permanent, not by what is transitory. The principle of hierarchical ministry is thus oriented to the search for unity, not by a vertical command structure, but by reason of the Church's nature and its evangelizing mission (*AG* 2.35; *EN* 59), just as the magisterium is at the service of the Word of God and not the reverse (*DV* 10).

The fact that the hierarchical ministry belongs to a few (*PO* 2) does not exclude those few from being included among all the *Christifideles*. The Council, in speaking of a difference "in essence and not merely degree," wanted to avoid attributing any trace of superiority to the ministerial priesthood with respect to the common priesthood (*LG* 10). This phrase, which remains controversial, should be understood as referring to a difference *within the common priesthood*. In other words, the ordained minister exercises a specific function or ministry by reason of the sacrament of orders, by which he is ordained primarily to serve the community and not to perform worship (*PO* 8; *LG* 28–29). Due to its sacramental character, the ministerial priesthood is subordinated to the *universitas fidelium*.

Thus, the common priesthood of the faithful is prior and permanent; it is never lost. Moreover, it is a prerequisite for attaining and exercising the ministerial priesthood. In summary, "the Vatican has made an option: its starting point is not the celebration of the Eucharist [worship] but the *mission of the people of God*, which implies recognizing the ontological priority of the priestly people, within which priestly ministry is inscribed."[8] Consequently, the common priesthood constitutes the totality of *Christifideles* as a *priestly community or people*[9] in and *for* whom the hierarchical ministry is exercised.

EPISCOPAL COLLEGIALITY AND PRIMACY

The difficulty in receiving synodality as a new configuring hermeneutic for all the ecclesial subjects is clearly manifested in the still unresolved juxtaposition in defining the relations between collegiality and primacy. These relations are understood in terms of subordination and support, a conception that has hampered the achievement of an *organic reform of ecclesial subjects, mentalities, and structures* (UR 4, 6). The two subjects are presented as entities that can act separately from the people of God but in close relationship with each other; they are therefore not defined by their reciprocal interaction with the rest of the faithful nor in the light of an ecclesiology of the local churches. In consequence, the sense of the faithful—*sensus fidei*—is neither binding nor mandatory for the exercise of their mission.

This problem results from the concept of *college* in the conciliar debates. Pressured by the conservative minority to save the doctrine of primacy promulgated at Vatican I, Paul VI added a "Preliminary Note of Explanation" (PNE) to *Lumen Gentium*, in which he states,

> As Supreme Pastor of the Church, the Supreme Pontiff can always exercise his power at will, as his very office demands. Though it is always in existence, the College is not as a result permanently engaged in *strictly* collegial activity....Rather, it acts as a college in the strict sense only from time to time and *only with the consent of its head.* (PNE 4)

Although the Preliminary Note of Explanation is not an integral part of the Council documents and therefore cannot be taken as a hermeneutical criterion for the interpretation of *Lumen*

Gentium, it has influenced postconciliar understanding of collegiality and its exercise.[10] It gave rise to an equivocal reception of *LG* and ensured that the relations between the episcopal institutions and the papacy adhered to a model of service to the primacy by reason of its "personal" authority. This was clear from the way Paul VI conceived of the new institutions. In his view, for example, "the Roman Curia is the instrument the Pope needs and uses to fulfill his own divine mandate," and the Synod of Bishops is "a stable council of Bishops for the universal Church, directly and immediately subject to Our authority."[11] Moreover, the *motu proprio Sollicitudo Omnium Ecclesiarum* stated that the Bishop of Rome has "full, supreme, and universal power and can exercise it freely."[12]

The doctrine of episcopal collegiality, a great novelty of the Council, was thus born under this cloud, stressing the difference between ecclesial subjects more than the need for respectivity and reciprocity. If the collegial relationship is understood in terms of service and assistance to the primacy, the door is left open for collegial practice that is affective rather than effective and, therefore, not binding on the Bishop of Rome. Collegial affection consists in bonds of communion and fraternity. We might say that the 1985 Extraordinary Synod institutionalized the practice of "affective" collegiality within the hierarchy's communion with the papacy, thus putting aside the "effective" collegiality that is horizontal and binding, and oriented toward achieving ecclesial consensus that leads to structural reforms in the Church.

This juxtaposition produced, in turn, a hermeneutical change in the understanding and practice of participation and coresponsibility among all the ecclesial subjects, not just the bishops and the pope. Coresponsibility was not understood any more as an essential relationship that completes the others, but as an auxiliary relationship, offering assistance that does not define the essence and mission of each subject in respectivity to the others.

Referring to the decree *Christus Dominus* (no. 4), the constitution *Lumen Gentium* defines collegiality in the context of the relations of power between the episcopal college and the primacy, and it stresses the communion of the college members among themselves and with the pope (*LG* 22). The bishops' identity with respect to the local churches was not a factor in conceiving the nature of the episcopacy. The definition adopted is clear from the following hermeneutical sequence:

(a) "Just as in the Gospel, the Lord so disposing, Saint Peter and the other apostles constitute one apostolic college, so in a similar way the Roman Pontiff, the successor of Peter, and the bishops, the successors of the apostles, are joined together."

(b) "One is constituted a member of the Episcopal body in virtue of sacramental consecration and hierarchical communion with the head and members of the body."

(c) "This college, insofar as it is composed of many, expresses the variety and universality of the People of God, but insofar as it is assembled under one head, it expresses the unity of the flock of Christ." (*LG* 22)

Several elements that contribute to a definition of episcopal collegiality emerge from this hermeneutical sequence. First, the pope and the bishops belong to a single college, but are based on two different configurations or subjectivities: pope/Peter and bishops/apostles. Second, collegial unity is based on the equality of sacramental consecration and on the communion of the hierarchy with the primacy, such that the only efficient cause of the episcopacy is orders; this means that the episcopacy is not a subject derived from the primacy but enjoys the same supreme power. Third, the college and the pope together express the diversity of the people of God rather than themselves as isolated entities. This last aspect needs to be stressed to understand episcopal collegiality correctly.

While it is true that the first two elements of this sequence in *LG* 22 present the mutual relations between the college of bishops and the primacy of Rome as two ecclesial subjects united in *communio hierarchica* (can. 337; can. 333, §2), it is no less true that those relations occur within the framework of a totality in which the episcopal college expresses the entirety and the diversity of the people of God. If, as we have noted, chapter 2 of *Lumen Gentium* is normative for the interpretation of chapter 3—even with its stress on the verticality and the differences in the relations between primacy and college—it must be recognized that it is only *within* the people of God and *as Christifideles* by baptism that the pope and the bishops possess their identity and are qualified for exercising the mission of evangelization of the whole Church.

We can state, therefore, first, that a bishop's identity is established by being one of the *Christifideles*; and second, what differentiates the bishop with respect to the other faithful is in the proper exercise of the three offices of teaching, sanctifying, and governing (*LG* 21). The problem in the juxtaposition between episcopacy and primacy arises when ecclesial identities are defined based on what is incommunicable and distinctive by reason of the exercise of power, *potestas*, rather than on the reciprocity, complementarity, and coresponsibility that should characterize all the faithful. The papacy and the college have the same supreme power, but the college exercises it effectively only *with and under* Peter—*cum et sub Petro*—insofar as Peter is the head of the college. However, while the conciliar text recognizes that the bishops cannot act outside the framework of the totality constituted by the college, in which the pope is one more bishop, it does grant, at the same time, that the pontiff can act in a full, free, and universal manner, that is, in a personal manner apart from the episcopal college.

The problem thus created does not actually derive from *Lumen Gentium*; it comes rather, as we explained above, from the addition of the Preliminary Explanatory Note, which cannot be recognized as a text of the Council, as explained, and created an unresolved juxtaposition. It is there that one reads that the pope can act "according to his own judgment or discretion" (*propia discretio*) and "at will" (*ad placitum*); he can "proceed according to his own discretion in arranging, promoting, and approving the exercise of collegial activity." If the Note is understood as the criterion for interpreting *Lumen Gentium*, then the primacy is placed above the episcopal college.

This unresolved juxtaposition between primacy and collegiality has given rise to a subordinate relationship that has not helped synodal reform. The juxtaposition (*LG* 22) can only be overcome if we situate both subjects—bishops and pope—within the hermeneutic framework that synodality offers us, with the spirit of achieving the "healthy decentralization" (*EG* 16) and cosharing of power[13] that is proper to a synodal model of Church, as we have previously explained and insisted.

While collegiality refers to the nature and form proper to the episcopacy as it is exercised among bishops with and under Peter (see *LG* 22–23),[14] synodality is instead *a constitutive mark of the whole of ecclesial life*; it is *the whole Church's way of proceeding*, and, therefore, it involves the totality of the people of God.[15] Consequently, collegiality must be conceived and understood on the basis of synodality, and not vice versa. This is the path toward the declericalization of *ecclesial practices and structures*, a task that "bishops and priests can in no way accomplish by themselves."[16] As Francis notes, "It is impossible to think of a conversion of our activity as a Church that does not include the active participation of all the members of God's People"[17] as fruit of an essential coresponsibility.

Even here the words of Bishop De Smedt can help us recover an important hermeneutical key when he points out that, in the *mens* of the Council, "collegiality is the *active cooperation* of the whole episcopal order with the Roman Pontiff in the *pastoral care of the people of God*." Thus, even if the college acts in hierarchical communion with the primacy, both must act in close connection with *pastoral care*. This means that they must be acting precisely as bishops of local churches, carrying out the mission of evangelization in their capacity as pastors of the people of God situated in a particular locality.

It is helpful to recall, here, the words of Cardinal Suenens when, in reference to the responsibility and exercise of this pastoral care, he insisted that it was not exclusively of the bishops. He warned,

> It was the understanding of this [lay] identity that inspired the Council to create in every diocese in the world a diocesan pastoral council composed of priests, religious and lay people in order to utilize and express the reality of their coresponsibility....The laity must help in elaborating the general orientation of pastoral activity within a diocese, a sphere of life or a parish. Because of their professions and their daily experience, lay people know how to draw the greatest profit from teamwork.[18]

Coresponsibility is not *secondary* and cannot be understood as a subordinate relationship among ecclesial subjects; it does not come into play only in relation to the world. Rather, it is an *essential* element and must involve all the faithful in all the stages of the process of elaboration of pastoral decisions, for they are the agents of the Church's evangelizing mission. To fully achieve this, an organic revision of the current Code of Canon Law will be needed. Structures such as the diocesan and the parish pastoral councils should be mandatory and assumed as concrete mediations where all ecclesial subjects, without exemption or exclusion, should exercise their baptismal right to listen, discern, elaborate, and evaluate decisions together in a communal act. Furthermore, if we take a more comprehensive revision of Canon Law according to the normative character of the Church as people of God in *Lumen Gentium* and the subsequent exercise of the essential coresponsibility of all the *faithful*, it is necessary, as Carlos Schickendantz explains,

> to give more vigor to the statute of the Dioceses and to the establishment of the Bishops within the People of God. Along these lines are suggestions made by various authors: revitalize Diocesan Councils and Synods; review the procedure for the selection and appointment of bishops; ordaining the new bishops in their own Cathedrals, in the midst of their people; symbolically enrich the rite of welcoming the new Bishop if he has already been ordained; significantly reduce the ordinations of Bishops for official or administrative positions, etc.[19]

By this way of proceeding, the decisions taken by the ecclesial authority will always represent the *consensus ecclesiae* and can be accountable to all the faithful. Synodal structures are driven by *ecclesiogenetic processes* that configure the ecclesial *we*—as expressed by the International Theological Commission and developed by Serena Noceti[20]—thus putting into motion permanent practices that lead to conversion and reform.

7

Ecclesiogenesis

To advance a synodal reception of the Council's ecclesiology, we must consider how to *reconfigure* ourselves as the people of God. This step should lead to reform of the identity and vocation of the ordained ministry and the hierarchy, as propounded above, and to recognition of the laity as a fully ecclesial subject, a recognition that has still not been fully achieved in the Church. Such recognition means much more than participation (or not) in a synod or a pastoral council; it involves the *synodalization* of the whole Church.

A *synodal reconfiguration* of the ecclesiastical institution requires both recognition of the hermeneutical primacy of the order expounded in chapter 2 of *Lumen Gentium* and acceptance of the binding character of the *sensus fidei fidelium* for establishing the *consensus omnium fidelium*. To that end, it is necessary to design relational and communicational dynamics that integrate all the ecclesial subjects as *Christifideles* so that they can listen, discern, elaborate, and make decisions together. In this way, the *sensus ecclesiae totius populi* will find expression, and not only the *sensus ecclesiae* of the hierarchy. Given that the people of God is the only subject of the Church and that all the faithful are core-sponsible by reason of baptism, it is essential that all participate in the pastoral care. Beginning with these elements, we can imagine the new steps toward a synodal ecclesiality, and we can evaluate some of those already taken in that direction.

THE EXPANSION OF EPISCOPAL COLLEGIALITY

Having defined the nature and exercise of collegiality only in its relation to the primacy, and not as part of an ecclesiology of the local churches, Paul VI saw a fuller realization of the college in the institution of the Synod of Bishops.[1] This new structure reinforced the idea of a hierarchical episcopal collegiality that is exercised strictly *with* and *among* some (the bishops) and *for* one (the pope). This perspective now needs revision so as to integrate it into a larger framework, one that involves our walking *together* by reason of the coresponsibility of all the *faithful* as subjects, as well as *for* the evangelizing mission of the whole Church. Some steps in this direction are evident in the way Francis has conceived the Synod of Bishops: he has inserted it into the *sensus fidei* of the entire people of God and placed it at the service of the faithful (mission) and not just of the primacy.

There is a problem in interpreting synodality only as a renewed way of exercising episcopal collegiality. It should not be understood simply as an expansion of Paul VI's conception, which saw in the Synod of Bishops the ideal form of collegiality. Francis, with a more inclusive vision, has stated that "the Synod of Bishops, representing the Catholic episcopacy, is transformed into an expression of episcopal collegiality within an entirely synodal Church [and] inspires all ecclesial decisions."[2] We can appreciate the steady process of expansion of the exercise of episcopal collegiality through an episcopal structure like the Synod of Bishops, into which is inserted the people of God, but not the reverse. Thus, *Episcopalis Communio* states, "Although structurally it is essentially configured as an episcopal body, this does not mean that the Synod exists separately from the rest of the faithful. On the contrary, it is a suitable instrument to *give voice* to the entire People of God" (no. 6).

In this context, synodality aims to achieve greater integration and interaction between the hierarchy and the rest of the faithful through the Synod, understood as an institutional mediation that articulates "the ministry of the personal and collegial exercise of apostolic authority" with "the synodal exercise of discernment on the part of the community."[3] This is done in part through extensive processes of consultation and through greater involvement of the faithful in the Church's discernment and decision-making, always taking as a reference and finality the better functioning of the episcopal structures.

In the vision of Francis, synodality appears to combine two great subjects. On the one hand, there is the collective subject that becomes concretized in "the exercise of the *sensus fidei* of the *universitas fidelium* (all)," including all those who are heard prior to the celebration of a Synod. On the other hand, we have "the ministry of leadership of the college of Bishops, each with his own presbyterium (some) and the ministry of unity of the Bishop and the bishop of Rome (one)."[4] The goal must be to achieve better articulation between the people of God (all) and the hierarchy (collegiality) by taking into account three elements: "the communitarian aspect that includes the whole people of God, the collegial dimension that is part of the exercise of episcopal ministry, and the primatial ministry of the Bishop of Rome."[5]

Ecclesiogenesis

Even with the integration of the hierarchy into the people of God, an episcopal model is still maintained: it is made up "of bishops" and has a "consultative" character with respect to the primacy. The bishop cannot and should not walk solely with his peers; he is called to walk with all the faithful in his capacity as pastor of a portion of the Church in the locality to which he belongs and which he serves as one more of the faithful. If our aim is to reform the structure and the purpose of the Synod of Bishops, then the exercise of episcopal collegiality needs to be inserted within the ecclesiology of the local churches.

A bishop cannot attend a Synod simply to give his individual opinion; rather, he must sound out and express the opinions of the faithful or the *sensus fidei* of his church. This helps to reconfigure the Synod within the framework of the *communio ecclesiarum*. However, the solution must not be oriented toward a reform of the Institution of the Synod of Bishops, for it will continue to be an episcopal structure. The challenge is to create new synodal structures in a synodalized Church.

Even if this third millennium allows for a renewed practice of episcopal collegiality, we must still ask whether the structure of the Synod of Bishops will be maintained as a reference. If such is the case, it would perhaps be wise to create a formula that is *ecclesial* and not *episcopal*. Today, however, the completely new definition of the Church that Paul VI requested means much more than episcopal reform: it requires reconceiving, and not merely modifying, the forms by which all Church structures and mentalities can be effectively *synodalized*. If synodality is a new constitutive dimension that affects "everyone and everything" in the Church, it cannot be limited to a consultative method of listening and discerning; still less can it be defined as simple improvement of an episcopal structure. For even when nonbishops are allowed to vote, the fundament and the finality continue to be *episcopal*, both in their identity and in their vocation and functioning.

It is therefore important to recognize that synodality, as a constitutive dimension, is more than a synod, and it is also more than a mere method: it is a principle, and it is a hermeneutics of reconfigured relations and communicative dynamics among all ecclesial subjects that sets in motion an integral, organic transformation of the whole Church. It brings about an ecclesiogenesis that challenges us to discern the identities and vocations of all ecclesial subjects and structures under the rubric of the *ecclesial "we"* of the people of God. This challenge is undoubtedly at the heart of what it means to build consensus in the Church.

Conceiving the Church as the people of God and building the ecclesial "we," as we have been advocating, requires a reform of the theology of ordained ministry: episcopal collegiality must be reconceived in a synodal key and opened to the participation and baptismal coresponsibility of all the faithful. It is not a question of who votes or does not vote in a Synod of Bishops; it is much more than that. The issue is organic, and it permeates the exercise of authority and power, which are understood to be a *shared service* thanks to a new conception of the modes of interaction of all the faithful at all levels of the Church.

In this model, the last word cannot be taken in isolation by *some* (bishops) or by *one* (pope); rather, it is spoken only after there is a *consensus* of all the faithful, among whom are the pope and the bishops, who participate in the whole process and do not just come in at the end, when decisions are made. There is a need to understand better the teaching of *Dei Verbum* 10, according to which the Word of God has been entrusted to "the entire People of God united with their shepherds" so that together they can "achieve a single consensus" (*fidelium conspiratio*) and establish an essential, reciprocal, and thus binding relation between the *sensus fidei* and magisterium.

What this means today is that reforming the exercise of power involves a procedure that unfolds in connection with the faithful, as stated clearly by Cardinal Suenens:

> The episcopacy, for its part, is not a self-sufficient oligarchy sufficient unto itself. It understands itself in its vital twofold relationship: with its head, on the one hand, and with the entire *presbyterium* and all the laity, on the other.…We can now say that the Second Vatican Council certainly was characterized by a move in the direction of *democratization* because of the accent it placed on the people of God, by the stress it laid on the hierarchy as a service, and by its creation of certain organisms within the church which favor democratic methods of government. History teaches us that, while the structure of the church is hierarchical by the very will of its founder, the ways of exercising authority in the church have varied throughout the centuries.[6]

This democratic element, which involves the ways in which an institution operates, is described with precision by the canonist Corecco:

> Ultimately the problem of power within the People of God…is simply that of the nature of the relationship between the bishops and other Christians at the level of operations and decisions; consequently, it has to do with the ways in which the clergy and laity participate in responsibility that belongs to the successors of the apostles in the Christian proclamation in the world.[7]

Thus far, we can see that with Francis the exercise of episcopal collegiality has been expanded through a synodal dynamic. Today, we can speak of a *synodal collegiality*, which does not mean a reform of ordained ministry or collegiality or episcopal structures as such, but rather a recovery of the theology of the *sensus fidei* that was not readily accepted after the Council.[8] In the words of the International Theological Commission, this form of synodal collegiality is presented "on the basis of the doctrine of the *sensus fidei* of the People of God and the sacramental collegiality of the episcopate in hierarchical communion with the Bishop of Rome." This statement presupposes a synthesis of three elements that have contributed to the work throughout the current pontificate: (a) the creation of the link between "the communitarian aspect that includes the whole people of God, the collegial dimension that is part of the exercise of episcopal ministry, and the primatial ministry of the bishop of Rome"; (b) the promotion of "the baptismal dignity and coresponsibility of all … [and at the same time] the specific ministry of pastors in collegial and hierarchical communion with the bishop of Rome"; and (c) the promotion of a collaborative dynamic "on the level of communion of the local churches in a region and on the level of communion of all the Churches in the universal Church." This is so because "synodality involves the exercise of the *sensus fidei* of the *universitas fidelium* (all), the ministry of leadership of the college of Bishops, each one with his presbyterium (some), and the ministry of unity of the Bishop of Rome (one)."[9]

Even so, having advanced in synodal collegiality, we must also be aware that, if synodality is a constitutive mark of the Church, it cannot be reduced to the institution of the Synod, or to an assembly, as we have noted. The objective of the Synod of Bishops is to bring together bishops from all over the world to advise the Roman primate (CIC, can. 342), without the advice given being in any way binding on the final decision of the pope. Although the Code of Canon Law gives the pontiff the ability to concede a deliberative and binding force to the decision of the bishops (CIC, can. 343), the episcopal institution continues to be a body of collaboration and consultation that expresses only affective collegiality (*Christus Dominus* 5). For this to change and become effective, the pope would have to *ratify and promulgate* the conclusions reached by the synodal fathers. Francis mentioned this possibility in *Episcopalis Communio*, but he has not yet exercised it:

> § 1. Once the Final Document of the Assembly is approved by the members, it is presented to the Roman Pontiff, who decides about its publication. If it is expressly approved by the Roman Pontiff, the Final Document becomes part of the ordinary Magisterium of the Successor of Peter. § 2. If the Roman Pontiff grants the Assembly of the Synod deliberative powers, according to canon 343 of the Code of Canon Law, the Final Document becomes part of the ordinary Magisterium of the Successor of Peter once it has been *ratified* and promulgated by him. In this case the Final Document is published with the signature of the Roman Pontiff along with the signatures of the members. (*EC* 18)

The Synod for the Amazon is a fine example of the praxis of synodal dynamics. That process involved, first, "listening to all the faithful" and not only to the bishops or episcopal conferences. Tens of thousands of persons and hundreds of institutions were consulted in preparing for the Synod. Second, "communal discernment processes were carried out" in two phases: first, in local and regional assemblies convened prior to the Synod to produce the instrument of labor, and then in the Synodal Assembly itself, with the participation of voting and nonvoting members. Third, the "interpretation proper to the episcopal college" led to the "final decision" made by the pope, who participated as one more faithful, or one more synodal father, even though this figure is not yet institutionalized.[10]

As noted, a further aspect of synodal collegiality, still awaiting implementation, is found in *Episcopalis Communio* 18, which allows the pontiff to ratify and promulgate the Synod's final document as part of the Church's ordinary teaching. While this has not happened explicitly, it appears embryonically in *Querida Amazonia*, the post-synodal apostolic exhortation. The pope made it clear that *Querida Amazonia* does not replace the *Final Document* of the Synod (*QA* 2) but rather "assumes it" (no. 3). He further recommended that the Final Document be read in its entirety (no. 3) and then applied in the local churches (no. 4).

All this suggests that we find ourselves in a moment of ecclesiogenesis: we are being encouraged to take a new leap, from the "collegial 'we' of the episcopate gathered in unity *cum Petro et sub Petro*"[11] to the "ecclesial 'we' where every 'I,' clothed in Christ (cf. Gal 3:27), lives and journeys with his or her brothers and sisters as a responsible and active agent of the one mission of the People of God."[12] A deepening of our understanding of *episcopal collegiality*—the great novelty of the Council—and its relation to *synodal collegiality*—the contribution of Francis's pontificate—must advance even further; it must progress toward a new way of proceeding, that of *synodal ecclesiality*, whose mission is to re-create identities and communicational dynamics between ordained and nonordained ministry, between the common priesthood of the faithful and the ministerial priesthood.

A first step would be putting into practice the call of *Apare-cida*, as we noted, that "the laity participate in [ecclesial] *discernment, decision making, planning*, and *execution*" (*Aparecida* 371). For this purpose, the hierarchy must create concrete mediations, "making use of the participatory bodies provided by law, without excluding any other modality that it deems appropriate" (*EC* 6). The result should be that everyone, "'from the bishops to the last of the lay faithful,' give their universal consent in matters of faith and morals" (no. 5).

In short, it is necessary to implement original ways of proceeding that, as already noted, have "their starting point and also their point of arrival in the People of God" (*EC* 7). This step presumes the recognition of the laity as a *subject*, a major shift that has still not come full circle. Such recognition will depend mostly on the reform of the ordained ministry, the manner of elaborating consensus, and finally, the adoption of a model for sharing the decision-making power in the Church.[13]

THE LAITY AS A SUBJECT

If we follow the conciliar *mens*, the participation of all the faithful equally in the common priesthood offers the hermeneutical framework for conceiving the communicational and relational dynamics that should exist in the Church between ordained and nonordained ministers. This theme appears already in the first drafts of *Apostolicam Actuositatem* that refer us to the common priesthood, which grants to all "the right, the honor, and the duty to exercise the Church's apostolate in the proper way."[14] The lay state is presented as a *proper way* to exercise the common priesthood and to participate in the priesthood of Christ. This participation, as expressed in the *textus prior*, occurs in different *ways and degrees.*[15] In other words, the participation is not delegated or defective but is a proper life condition that differs "essentially" from hierarchical ministry. The use of the word *diversitas* in the conciliar text emphasizes this essential distinction to highlight the specificity of each ecclesial identity[16] under the rubric of "diversity of ministries and unity of mission" (*AA* 2). The specificity, here, neither excludes nor isolates.

This is the first time that laypeople have been recognized as subjects, with their own particular but differentiated way of living the common condition of the baptized as *Christifideles*. Laypersons are not simply the faithful, since this condition is *common* to all subjects within the totality of *Christifideles* that constitute the people of God (*LG* 32). The lay state is one way of realizing the Christian vocation and of participating actively, distinctively, and coresponsibly in the Church's mission (*SC* 14) *suo modo... pro sua parte* (*LG* 31). It is defined not by the clerical condition, but by charity (*diakonia* to the world) and by preaching (*martyria*). The lay vocation is neither delegated nor derived, much less residual.

Lumen Gentium provides two fundamental keys to understanding a theology of the laity. It first defines lay identity negatively and incorrectly: "The term laity is here understood to mean all the faithful except those in holy orders and those in the state of religious life specially approved by the Church" (*LG* 31). The contradiction appears when the lay state is defined in a contrasting, residual way, as a condition of life that lacks holy orders and so has no power. The second key offered by *Lumen Gentium* is positive; it recognizes what is common to all *Christifideles* when it defines the identity of the laity as follows:

> These faithful are by baptism made one body with
> Christ and are constituted among the People of

Ecclesiogenesis

God; they are in their own way made sharers in the priestly, prophetical, and kingly functions of Christ; and they carry out for their own part the mission of the whole Christian people in the Church and in the world. (*LG* 31)

Laypeople are not simply believers, and the lay state is not merely a basic condition of Christian existence; it is a *special way* of being *faithful*. *Apostolicam Actuositatem* provides an interpretive key for overcoming the contradiction between these definitions: it refers us to the logic of the *universitas fidelium*, which includes all the faithful equally—bishops, clergy, religious, and laity. If this sense of the *totality of the faithful* is the hermeneutical principle that defines all the different ecclesial identities, it follows that "the apostolate of the laity and the pastoral ministry *complete each other*" (*AA* 6). Both share in the apostolic character of all the Church's members, so that the layperson is considered an "authentic apostle" (no. 6). *Lumen Gentium* states,

The pastors know how much the laity contribute to the welfare of the entire Church. They also know that they were not ordained by Christ to take upon themselves alone the entire salvific mission of the Church toward the world. On the contrary they understand that it is their noble duty to shepherd the faithful and to recognize their ministries and charisms, so that all according to their proper roles may cooperate in this common undertaking with one mind. (*LG* 30)

To read *Apostolicam Actuositatem* or chapter 4 of *Lumen Gentium* on the laity without interpreting it in the light of chapter 2 of *Lumen Gentium* on the people of God is to run the risk of

81

understanding this ecclesial identity in an individualist or fragmentary way; it is to see the laity as subordinate to the hierarchy and as residual with respect to the sacramental order. Furthermore, a reductionist reading of the notion of *Christifideles* would deny that laypeople are a *proper* and *binding* subject for defining the nature and the exercise of the other ecclesial identities. Hence, we see the importance of the hermeneutical principle established in *Lumen Gentium*: "Everything that has been said above concerning the People of God is intended for the laity, religious, and clergy alike" (no. 30).[17]

Thus, laypersons live ecclesiality—*ad intra* and *ad extra*—but they do so because of their "secular character," which is neither sacramental nor clerical. They live ecclesiality as *witnesses* who announce the "kingdom" and make it present in the world (*LG* 31) as they seek to transform society (*AA* 10). The sociological reality of the world, in all its dimensions, is assumed theologically and reconfigured christologically by the laity through their mission of being a bridge between the Church and the world, as followers of Jesus and builders of the kingdom in the world.[18]

Here, we must highlight the importance of the *sensus fidei* (*LG* 12), which is the operating principle that binds all the faithful on the basis of what each person contributes to the whole of the people of God, while always seeking harmony (*GS* 92). This same principle applies to religious life, which "is not an intermediate state between the clerical and lay states" (*LG* 43); rather, it is another ecclesial identity that, as *faithful*, embodies the charismatic witness of the Christian vocation.[19]

The path traced thus far allows us to delineate the hermeneutical logic that emerges clearly in *LG* 9–12. In the Church as "People of God" (no. 9), "the common priesthood of the faithful and the ministerial or hierarchical priesthood are interrelated:

each of them in its own special way is a participation in the one priesthood of Christ" (no. 10); each of them is called "to holiness" (no. 11) and to "share in Christ's prophetic office" (no. 12). While the ecclesial subjects are active as the faithful, they are so within the framework of their belonging to the people of God *as a whole*. However, there is still a long way to go because full participation and coresponsibility raise the question of who participates in the structures.

We cannot deny that some structures of participation for the laity and the nonordained ministry already exist. Some are of a permanent nature, such as pastoral councils and economic committees. Others are more dynamic and transitory, such as parish assemblies, meetings between various pastoral zones, and diocesan assemblies. Some proposals made by the Council were not even incorporated into the Code of Canon Law. One example, recommended in *Apostolicam Actuositatem*, is the Council of Lay People, a body that would have clergy, religious, and laity work together at all levels—parochial, diocesan, national, and international (*AA* 26). It would differ from the Diocesan Pastoral Council in that its members would relate to one another simply as faithful and not according to their hierarchy. Finally, pastoral experiences have also emerged that propose new models of collaboration in community leadership, such as the *collaborative ministry* in English-speaking countries, the *pastoral teams* in French-speaking countries, or the proposal establishing a group of *itinerant priests* in Latin America. Such models, however, have rarely been implemented.

Furthermore, where collaborative models have been established, it is important to consider who controls and participates in them. The question about the type of persons participating is crucial because it will shape the relational and communicational dynamics involved in the listening and discerning processes, and ultimately in the construction of the ecclesial identity. Recognizing that there are many subjectivities in the Church is the basis for reflecting not only on *who* participates in the processes of elaborating and making decisions but also and above all on *how* the decisions are construed and made binding.[20]

One concrete case of listening, very pertinent today, involves taking seriously the question about the participation of women in the Church. Referring to coresponsibility, Cardinal Suenens recalled what had been requested in Rome in 1967, during the Third World Congress of the Lay Apostolate:

> The Third World Congress of the Lay Apostolate formulates the desire to see granted to woman all the rights and all the responsibilities of the Christian within the Catholic Church, and that a serious doctrinal study be undertaken on the place of woman in the sacramental order and in the Church. The congress asks moreover: (1) that competent women be made part of all pontifical commissions; (2) that qualified women be consulted with regard to the revision of the canon law, especially those that concern women, in order that feminine dignity be fully recognized and that the greatest possibilities in the service of the Church be granted to woman. The role of woman is not yet fully recognized; it is a goal yet to be achieved.[21]

If this project is to bring about not only a change of mentality but also a change of structures and modes of governance, it must "encourage and develop the means of participation proposed in the Code of Canon Law and other forms of pastoral dialogue, out of a desire to listen to everyone and not simply to those who would tell [the bishop] what he would like to hear" (*EG* 31). To advance the recognition of the laity today, there must be a clearer definition of the spaces and the modes of the laity's participation in ecclesial structures. This participation touches the very heart of the involvement of this ecclesial subject in the life and the mission of the Church. A concrete example is their participation or nonparticipation in the deliberative moments of a synodal process, as explained by Dianich:

> The common faithful can determine the decisions to be taken, if they are members of an Association of the faithful or of an institute of Consecrated Life, or even in a Society of Apostolic Life. However, in the diocese and parish where ordinary ecclesial life flows, lay people do not enjoy any position in which with their votes can effectively determine, even in matters that do not directly pertain to the charism of the ordained ministry, the decisions concerning the ordinary life of the community. This weakness of the *Code* is, to say the least, not due to dogmatic imperatives.[22]

This is a challenge that needs to be addressed if we want to contribute to reconfiguring the Church in a synodal key, from bottom to top, in ways that affect everyday life. We should start by discerning the synodalization of the whole Church, which requires the creation of a link between the *sensus fidei* and the *consensus omnium fidelium*. New styles and organizational practices in the Church must be inspired by the classic principle: "*What affects everyone must be treated and approved by everyone.*"[23] For this reason, "[implementing] greater synodality requires correct application of the canonical provisions, proper understanding of the decision-making modalities, and profound trust in the People of God that involves them in the preparation of decisions to be made by the pastors in order to realize the missionary dream of reaching one and all (*EG* 31)."[24] This implies a synodal ecclesiality that pervades mentalities, processes, and structures.

8

The Challenge of
Synodal Ecclesiality

LINKING *SENSUS FIDEI* AND
CONSENSUS OMNIUM FIDELIUM

The novelty of this new way of proceeding is expressed in the institutional reconfiguration of synodal ecclesiality or the building of the ecclesial "we," for "synodality is an essential dimension of the Church, which through it reveals and configures herself as the pilgrim People of God and as the assembly convoked by the risen Lord."[1] If the path of *reconfiguration* goes beyond *synodal collegiality* and embraces the form of *synodal ecclesiality*, we need to face the ongoing challenge of linking theologically the *sensus fidei* with the *consensus omnium fidelium*. It is not about integrating the people of God into the hierarchy when participating in episcopal structures such as synods or bishops' conferences, but rather recognizing the hierarchs as members of the people of God, to whom they listen and with whom they live. As Archbishop De Smedt stated at the Council,

The teaching body does not rest exclusively on the Holy Spirit's action on the bishops; it [must] also *heed* the action of the same Spirit *on the people of God.* Therefore, the teaching body not only speaks to the People of God; it also *listens to this People* in whom Christ continues his teaching.[2]

The act of listening defines the very process of ecclesial life, for listening is part of the Church's vocation and mission, but "it is a reciprocal listening"[3] through the practice of the *sensus fidei,* which plays a normative role in the formation and exercise of all ecclesial identities, for it allows those identities to engage in the necessary reciprocity within the sole organic subject that is the people of God. Thus, we can say that while it is true that becoming the people of God (*EG* 113) is "the primary form of Christian communion,"[4] this goal cannot be achieved except through a *synodal* way of proceeding that is enabled by the doctrine of *sensus fidei.*[5] As Vitali explains,

> The doctrine of the *sensus fidei* rests on the conviction that the Spirit received in Baptism makes the believer capable of knowing and therefore of expressing meaningful things about the contents of the faith, to the extent that he lives the Christian experience: it is a kind of intuition, a knowledge by connaturality, a perception that is refined with the growth of life in Christ. The authority of the Church as *universitas fidelium* is based on this personal capacity.[6]

This involves giving primacy to the ecclesial form of knowing called *sensus fidei,*[7] which is a capacity given to every baptized person, but only when exercised as *sensus fidelium,* that is, within the totality of baptized persons in their mutual and communal inter-action. The core of the ecclesiological shift of the Council has to do with the notion of the *totality of the faithful*, which means that all the faithful are understood within a logic of reciprocity— never as a homogenized or uniform universal group—and each ecclesial subject is completed by the others. This is the teaching of Vatican II, which states,

> The *entire body of the faithful*, anointed as they are by the Holy One (cf. 1 John 2:20, 27), cannot err in mat-ters of belief. They manifest this special property by means of the whole people's supernatural discernment in matters of faith when 'from the Bishops down to the last of the lay faithful' they show universal agreement in matters of faith and morals. (*LG* 12)

The *sensus fidei fidelium* (sense of the faith on the part of the faithful) implies the recognition that all the *Christifideles* complete one another in relations of reciprocity and respectivity, as noted above. The whole or the totality of the faithful functions by integrat-ing and exercising the diversity of charisms, gifts, services, and min-istries that distinguish the people of God, and by orienting them all to the communal building of a *consensus ecclesiae*. It is this communal act that seals and grants authority to the *consensus ecclesiae* reached by all the *Christifideles* when interacting as a whole and, furthermore, it is this communal decision, of all the *faithful*, that mediates the correct comprehension of the *depositum fidei* ("the body of revealed truth in the Scriptures and Tradition") according to each time and epoch. Peter Hünermann offers, here, a key interpretation:

> When it is a matter of understanding and interpreting the *depositum fidei*, or of questions of faith and morals

arising from the *depositum fidei*, then reason, illuminated by faith, has the competence to decide about these questions. If the decision is accepted by the community of believers as a whole, then it has the seal of validity: in the given circumstances, in the present historical situation, presupposing the general forms and conditions of knowledge and thought, the decision should be seen in this way and no other. The *consensus ecclesiae* confirms it. Believers can then also be confident that, in following this decision, they are not betraying the faith as it is affirmed in the *depositum fidei* but are genuinely adhering to it. Thus, a decision agreed upon in this way opens access to the infallibility of the *depositum fidei*. Since the decisions of the Church mediate access to the correct understanding of the *depositum fidei*, they are themselves essentially subordinate instances. The modifier "infallible" is applicable to them only in a subordinate, transferred, or analogous sense.[8]

Therefore, the belief of a single individual does not exist. The act of faith takes place *in* and *as* Church, in the form of the *sensus fidei ecclesiae*. However, as Rahner warned, a problem may arise when "groups are formed in such a way that they no longer really live together, pray together, or work with one another."[9] Isolated individuals or groups that object to a culture of encounter, meeting, coexistence, and sharing will not accept communal forms of living and interacting; they will be lacking in synodal attitudes.

From this perspective, we speak of *synodality* as a hermeneutics that enables and articulates the whole process of ecclesial reconfiguration of mentalities and structures. By continually forming specific identities within the totality of the people of God, it makes possible the infallibility *in credendo* of *all the faithful*, not only of one (primacy) or of some (collegiality). Therefore, the *sensus fidelium* and the magisterium are distinct but *complementary* subjects whose constant reciprocity produces and regulates the intelligence of faith. If this were not so, the *depositum fidei* would become an abstract, unilateral reality without any connection to the people of God.

The unity between these two subjects results not from the similar ways in which they exercise that function, but from the need of both subjects to be interrelated to achieve authentic *ecclesial consensus*. If the two subjects are complementary, the *consensus omnium fidelium* should be the fruit of a *sensus fidei totius populi*, the sense of the faith of all the people, and not of the *magisterium*. According to the Council (*DV* 10), all ecclesial subjects are called to interact within the principle of *singularis antistitum et fidelium conspiratio*, and it is in that communal interaction that the contents of faith are discerned and reinterpreted in the light of tradition and with the help of theological reflection from a particular context, thus producing something new.

Today, the *consensus omnium fidelium* needs to be exercised in a global Church,[10] and this requires the formation of synodal attitudes that will help the faithful to be aware of the diverse ways of understanding and proclaiming the gospel and to overcome all forms of cultural uniformity and homogeneity. While expressing and living Christianity, the faithful will become aware of the great multitude of actors that sustain the ecclesial structures, people who are diverse in terms of gender, experience, training, and culture. The complex interactions among them will give birth to a new sense of faith, and we will need better methods of communication so that listening, discernment, and consensus building can take place in this new synodal way of proceeding.[11]

Through this process, the act of listening cannot be limited to carrying out external consultations that are then analyzed by the hierarchy or a group of experts. Rather, the act of listening requires that the bishop be personally involved as *one of the faithful*, learning from the other participants and taking into consideration the diversity described above; he must engage in dialogue and share in discussion of differing points of view. He must be even more attentive when there are contrasting or opposed opinions, because the responsibility to express oneself and to listen to others flows from the charism given to every baptized person by the Spirit (*sensus fidei*).

It is in this context that discernment should take place because discernment will be ecclesial only when it is exercised within the setting of the *sensus fidelium*. It then takes the form of a *communal discernment* in which the whole body of the baptized interacts for the one purpose of achieving the *consensus fidelium*. Accordingly, all the faithful—understood as an organic body—must participate in these processes of communal discernment because, as Alphonse Borras notes,

> Discernment is not only done in the Church; *it makes the Church*, to the extent that it happens within the whole diversity of vocations, charisms, and ministries whereby the baptized hear the Word of God, examine the signs of the times, and participate in history under the action of the Holy Spirit. Discernment is an ecclesial process that requires the participation of all, each in their own way according to their level of interest and involvement. Discernment arises, in principle, from ecclesial synodality, but it requires translation into institutions, that is to say, places, instances, and organs in which it can be practiced in the Church.[12]

This complex process of interaction, which involves expressing, listening, discerning, and taking advice, links the *decision-making* process of *all*—people of God—with the *decision-taking* process of *many* (collegiality) and of *one* (primacy)—hierarchy. Even when synodality is enabled by our walking together and becomes real by our meeting and living this whole process together, it will become complete and fully realized only when *decisions are elaborated and made together* because "in the synodal Church the whole community, in the free and rich diversity of its members, is called together to pray, listen, analyze, dialogue, discern and offer advice on taking pastoral decisions which correspond as closely as possible to God's will."[13]

It is worth remembering here the golden rule of Saint Cyprian: "Nihil sine consilio vestro et sine consensu plebis mea privatim sententia gerere."[14] For this bishop, *taking advice* from the presbytery and *building consensus* with the whole people—including both the presbyters and the faithful—were fundamental to his episcopal ministry of keeping the people of God walking together in communion in the Church. He therefore used methods based on constant listening and dialogue to practice communal discernment, which allowed for the participation of all the faithful, not just priests, in deliberating on and making decisions. The first millennium thus offers the example of a *forma ecclesiae* in which the exercise of power was understood as shared responsibility.

The unity of the practices of expressing, listening, discernment, consulting, and decision-making enables a synodal process that creates a link between the *elaboration or making of decisions*, in which the whole of the people of God is involved as equal members of an ecclesial organism, and the *taking of decisions*, for which the bishops are responsible.[15] Following this model, "it would be better to say that the consultative bodies *elaborate* the decision, while the final responsibility for it falls to the pastoral authority that *assumes it*."[16] The emergence of this way of proceeding means devising models of ecclesial and episcopal cogovernance; there must be *shared power* that is exercised by all ecclesial subjectivities—*the faithful*—in a process of joint discernment. The International Theological Commission has clearly stated that "the synodal dimension of the Church must be brought out by enacting and directing discernment processes which bear witness to the dynamism of communion that inspires *all ecclesial decisions*."[17]

The key issue is the creation of a nexus based on "the circular relationship between the ministry of pastors, the participation and coresponsibility of lay people, and the stimulus coming from the charismatic gifts according to the dynamic circular link between 'one,' 'some,' and 'all.'"[18] This link expresses the full acceptance of the normative character of chapter 2 of *Lumen Gentium* for reconfiguring the Church as synodal. If, in accord with *Episcopalis Communio*, all the faithful participate in preparing for decisions, then *the making of decisions* will be an expression and implementation of the *consultation* on the part of the bishop, who has listened, discerned, taken advice, and accepted the counsel he was given in a synodal process according to the exercise of an essential, and not subordinated, coresponsibility.

Therefore, by situating the hierarchy within the people of God and understanding the latter as the principal and basic subject that encompasses everyone in the Church, the processes of discernment and decision-making are the responsibility of all the faithful, and not of the bishops and the pope alone. As Borras explains,

> In general, [the bishop] will act according to canon
> 127: he will not take issue with what the ecclesial

community has expressed unless there is significant reason. By virtue of their ordination and in accord with their office, the pastors will make the decisions. The making of decisions means that what was *developed jointly* is 'handed over to the Church'; the decision is in fact made by the authority of those who fulfill this role of articulation among the communities....According to this perspective, the pastors do not exercise their ministry in isolated fashion; they do so with the other faithful, and not without them. In this way *a communal modality in the exercise of ministry* is rediscovered.[19]

This does not affect the sacramentality of the episcopate but rather situates it and qualifies it in view of its character as transitory service defined by a coresponsible interaction and integration with all in the ecclesial body. The episcopate is therefore just *one faithful more*, even in the process of the evolution of doctrine,[20] because "the formal authority of an official post does not dispense the person exercising it...from the obligation of effectively procuring...the consent of those who are affected by a decision."[21] Therefore, the consensus is not a mere organizational matter or a redistribution of spaces and powers; rather, it is an *ecclesiological model* that entails the configuration of a new *synodal ecclesial identity*. This new identity implies the question about *power* and *authority* in the Church and discerns it according to the *good practices of shared power*. Here, we should recall the classical principle that "*what affects all should be discussed and approved by all*,"[22] especially since we sometimes forget the implications of the last part of the axiom.[23]

Shared responsibility is fundamental for a synodal Church in which "all can participate in solidarity, *through adequate channels and structures*."[24] Thus, whereas collegiality and papal primacy have their raison d'être in service to the people of God, it can be said that synodality "offers us the most adequate interpretative framework for understanding the hierarchical ministry itself."[25] And, as Serena Noceti reminds us, this will help the whole Church to "open up to the management of complex processes of community discernment that should involve parishes, presbyteries, and the faithful"[26] in general, as a continual and permanent practice, and as a process rather than a one-time event. It should thus be an ecclesial form and style of being and acting. We need to convert and relearn how to relate to each other, how to elaborate and take decisions together. We need to relearn practices of discernment and consensus building.

All these words may not be new to us, but in a synodal Church, they embody a new way of proceeding. Because it is new, we need to be open to conversion, and we need to learn from best practices found in the tradition of the Church, as well as in the contemporary sciences, such as sociology, psychology, and the study of governance.

THE SOCIOCULTURAL DYNAMICS OF THE *SENSUS POPULI*

Throughout his magisterium, Francis has used the notion of *sensus fidei* in two senses (*EG* 119; 197–201). He mentions it first in *Evangelii Gaudium* by referring to *Lumen Gentium* 12:

> In all the baptized, from first to last, the sanctifying power of the Spirit is at work, impelling us to evangelization. The people of God is holy thanks to this anointing, which makes it infallible *in credendo*. This means that it does not err in faith, even though it may

not find words to explain that faith….God furnishes
the totality of the faithful with an instinct of faith—
sensus fidei—which helps them to discern what is truly
of God. The presence of the Spirit gives Christians a
certain connaturality with divine realities, and a wisdom which enables them to grasp those realities intui-
tively, even when they lack the wherewithal to give
them precise expression. (*EG* 119)

But then he connects *Lumen Gentium* 12 with *Aparecida*,
understanding the totality of the faithful *as missionary disciples* and
highlighting this function as proper to the whole of the people of
God. *All* are subjects in the Church—not just the *many* nor the *one*
alone. Therefore, only by being and acting communally—*as all*—
can the people of God *not err*, enabling the infallibility *in credendo*.
By connecting *Aparecida* (nos. 186, 368) with *EG* (nos. 119, 120),
Francis can state that we become both "the faithful and missionary-
disciples" by virtue of baptism: being Christian presupposes inher-
iting and exercising these two conditions at the same time.

A second meaning of *sensus fidei* is found in the section of
Evangelii Gaudium dedicated to the *privileged place of the poor in
the people of God* (*EG* 197–201). This section treats of the nature
and the work, as well as the identity and the mission of the whole
Church. If the Church is *poor and for the poor*, its members and
its structures must allow themselves to be evangelized (*Aparecida*
99) by the poor, instead of being primarily concerned with evangelizing them. It is true that "the Church is an evangelizer, but she
begins by being evangelized herself….[She is] a Church which
is evangelized by constant conversion and renewal, in order to
evangelize the world with credibility" (*Evangelii Nuntiandi* 15).

Consequently, by making the poor the people of God's privileged subjects for exercising the ecclesial function of *sensus fidei*

(*EG* 198), Francis establishes the Church's option for the poor as a *normative mediation for listening to God* and *for discerning the mission* entrusted to us today. Thus, Francis is not only teaching that the model of Church as the people of God is "the primary form of Christian communion,"[27] but he is also pointing out the primary social space of that communion, since "the whole path of our redemption is marked by the poor" (*EG* 197).

Consequently, sensing the communication of God's wisdom through the poor makes it clear that we receive the communication and the salvation of God as a *people* and never as isolated individuals (*EG* 113). Since we always find God through mediations, through the words and gestures of the others, sensing faith implies "hearing, distinguishing and interpreting the many voices of our age" (*GS* 44). Here, Francis is applying John XXIII's principle of *pastorality*:

> Dividing this unity between listening to God and listening to our brothers and sisters is one of the great temptations experienced constantly by those of us who follow Jesus. And we must be aware of this. *The way we listen to our Father is same way we should listen to the faithful People of God.* If we don't listen with the same ears, the same receptivity, and the same heart, something is broken. Passing by without listening to the pain of our people, without rooting ourselves in their lives, in their land, is like listening to the Word of God without letting it take root in our depths and bear fruit. A plant, a history without roots, leads a thirsty life.[28]

We can therefore say that the ecclesial form of sensing, understanding, and living faith occurs in the context of our everyday life, but in the form of *sensus populi*. In other words, it happens within sociocultural relationships and in the context of the actual claims and needs that shape people's life (*GS* 1). *Sensus populi* inserts the practice and dynamics of *sensus fidei* and *sensus fidelium* in a *social place*.[29] *Sensus fidei* should be understood as the "personal subject" or capacity to know and express things about the contents of the faith, while the *sensus fidelium* is the "collective subject" or the exercise of the intelligibility of faith in a reciprocal interaction that occurs when all believers are together and thus create an event that enables them to listen to each other, and discern together in order to reach a consensus. Therefore, the totality of the faithful cannot be understood as a mere grouping of individuals, nor as an abstract or generic entity that cancels the personal identity of each subject. The concept expresses a *dynamic* in which the faithful complete one another in a real *social environment*, where faith is *essential* and is sensed and discerned *communally*. To speak of *sensus populi* helps to historicize the people's listening to God in the many faces and voices of our brothers and sisters, and the way in which this event is assimilated in the complex interaction of a community of faithful. All this serves to reveal the Church to the world as *a people who are building communion as they advance on a historical pilgrimage to God together*, as opposed to being asymmetrical, individual members of an organic, hierarchical institution (*EG* 111).

This ecclesial way of proceeding requires us to move beyond an unequal, clericalist Church, and to overcome a dualistic vision of the salvation and the world. As Cardinal Landázuri Ricketts advised during the Conference of Medellín in 1968,

> We are perhaps accustomed to a "clerical" view of the world. Sometimes we experience an almost spontaneous suspicion, distrust, or fear in the face of what

is called (I don't think very exactly) "the profane." Nevertheless, the Word of God became man and lives among us, thus giving meaning to everything human that exists and that happens. Therefore, *whenever we listen to other people, we listen to Christ; whenever we care about other people, we care about Christ; and to the extent that we meet with other people, learning how to commune with them, we meet with the same Lord.*[30]

The challenge, therefore, is to become the *people of God* walking together in *communion* in a fragmented and fractured world, and this entails believing as Christians that "no one is saved by himself or herself, individually, or by his or her own efforts. God attracts us by taking into account the complex interweaving of personal relationships entailed in the life of a human community" (*EG* 113). It is this perspective that channels Francis's reception of *Lumen Gentium* 12, as he clearly expressed in 2013:

An image of the Church that pleases me is that of a holy people, faithful to God. It is the definition I often use, and it is also the definition of *Lumen Gentium* in paragraph 12. Belonging to a people has a strong theological value: God, in the history of salvation, has saved a people. There is no full identity without belonging to a people. No one is saved alone, as an isolated individual, but God draws us to himself, taking into account the complex web of interpersonal relationships that are established in the human community. God enters into this dynamic of the people. The people are the subject. And the Church is the people of God traveling through history, with joys and sorrows.[31]

The Challenge of Synodal Ecclesiality

After all this reflection we can claim that our task for a true reform of the Church is not so much thinking about synodality as considering how to implement processes and create structures of effective synodalization of the whole Church in the light of Vatican II's theology of the *sensus fidei fidelium*. But this theology must be deepened with the principle of the *sensus fidei totius populi*, which enables a new ecclesial reconfiguration by affecting identities and communicative dynamics among all ecclesial subjects, as well as in all church structures *ad intra* and *ad extra*.

To speak about synodality is not a matter of understanding and modifying simple operational modes or methods that allow the ecclesial subjects to interact better with each other and with the world. It is rather to recognize a new way of being and doing Church, an ecclesiogenesis, in which the ecclesial ways of proceeding—spiritual, pastoral, institutional—make possible multiple and diverse theological-cultural institutional models and thus constitute the Church according to each epoch and culture.

All this implies, as we have seen throughout our reflection, that we are faced with the challenge of planning and advancing the theology and practice of episcopal collegiality, synodal collegiality, and synodal ecclesiality in the light of an organic and interconnected ecclesiological vision driven by the implementation of continual processes of synodalization of the whole Church as the people of God. In this sense, ecclesiology can only be understood as an ongoing process of ecclesiogenesis, as a permanent making of the Church and, in consequence, as a perennial reform.

This task will require genuine conversion of lifestyles and options, new practices of listening and discernment, collaborative ways of decision-making and decision-taking, and the creation or reform of structural mediations. All this must happen so that, while the specific contribution of hierarchical ministry is maintained, the unique and necessary contribution of laywomen and -men who offer their charisms, cultures, and specificities of gender are coresponsibly recognized and integrated into the whole life of the Church.

Decisive steps are required to assume synodality as a *constitutive ecclesial dimension* and *way of proceeding* for this third millennium, so that the Church can leave behind isolated forms of exercising authority and governing styles that are centralized and discretionary. In this sense, a process of synodalization of the whole Church begins at *the first level in the exercise of synodality,* that is, at the level of the *local churches* where the theological and cultural reconfiguration occurs. This implies, for the third millennium, the task of deepening and implementing the theological model of Church as people of God amid all the peoples of this earth (*LG* 13), and a communion lived as a *Church of churches* (*LG* 23).

We should evoke again the call of Pope Paul VI to find "a more complete definition of the Church." That is what synodality makes possible, by opening the path toward a synodalization of the whole Church, from bottom to top, and generating a process of theological-cultural configuring of local churches.

PART III

Synodality and the Local Churches

9

The Local Church

As we have noted, Pope Francis explains that "a synodal Church is a Church that listens." The implications of such an act of listening go beyond a personal conversion because the listening shapes the relations among ecclesial subjects and reconfigures the Church organization and structures. The act of listening to the people and their cultures enables a process of reconfiguration of the theological-cultural model of the ecclesial organization. Francis explains that the people of God must be listened to, in their particular place and time, in order to know "what the Spirit is saying to the churches" (Rev 2:7); by listening to the people, each Church can find ways of proceeding that respond to the particular locality where ecclesial life and mission evolves.

This is what the Synod for the Pan-Amazon Region claimed when it said that "[the Church] reconfigures her own identity through listening and dialoguing with the people, realities and stories of a [sociocultural] territory" (*Querida Amazonia* 66). As Vatican II insisted, listening should lead to discerning "in what way the customs, meaning of life and social order can be reconciled with the customs manifested by divine revelation" (*Ad Gentes* 22).

Therefore, the Church listens not simply to acquire more information, but to discern her mission and reach "a deeper accommodation in the whole sphere of Christian life" (*Ad Gentes* 22).

Adopting this ecclesiological perspective, the International Theological Commission states that "the first level on which synodality is exercised is the *Local Church*," precisely because "the historical, linguistic, and cultural links that mold interpersonal communication in the local Church and describe its particular features *facilitate the adoption of a synodal style*."[1] Consequently, a synodal way of proceeding implies that all local churches are called to develop "their own discipline, their own liturgical usage, and their own theological and spiritual heritage" (*LG* 23). It is, therefore, important to understand that synodality is the most appropriate way for the genesis of the processes of identity and theological-cultural reconfiguration of the Church under the model of the Church as *Church of Churches* presided over by the Bishop of the Church of Rome and in communion with all of them, thus fulfilling the *catholicity* of local churches.

Inspired in this ecclesiology, the Church has been summoned to a new Synod whose motto is *For a Synodal Church: Communion, Participation and Mission*. This new synodal path, lasting two years (from 2021 to 2023), will engage the entire Church in the task of discerning a new ecclesial model for the third millennium. Deepening the aggiornamento process initiated by Vatican II, the Synod wants to respond to the epochal ecclesial changes we are now experiencing. This may be the most important ecclesiological event in the current phase of reception of the Second Vatican Council. It will involve approximately 114 Episcopal Conferences of the Latin Rite, the Council of Eastern Catholic Patriarchs, six patriarchal Synods of the Eastern Churches, four major Archiepiscopal Synods, and five International Episcopal Councils. Deepening the ecclesiology of the people of God in the light of a model of Church of Churches, this new phase is recovering the Council's ecclesiology of the local churches and making it the normative starting point for a synodal Church. Through synodality, Francis is seeking to complete the unfinished reception of the Council regarding the priority of the local churches.

THE ECLIPSE OF THE ECCLESIOLOGY OF LOCAL CHURCHES

After Paul VI, there was a progressive deflation of the value of local cultures as normative for reinterpreting tradition, doing theology, and transmitting faith. In defining the local church, the formal element became weightier than the real one, so that a theological-cultural homogenization of ecclesial forms took place throughout the world. The local reality no longer played a key role in configuring the *actual* concrete forms of specific ecclesial entities. Primacy was conceded instead to the formal elements, that is, to the individual bishops, who were considered "the visible principle and foundation of unity in their particular churches," and to the celebration of the Eucharist as "the fount and apex of the whole Christian life" (*LG* 11).

From the 80s, centralism started to prevail in ecclesial governance and doctrinal development. This ecclesiological orientation was promoted through new documents of the magisterium, such as the apostolic constitution *Pastor Bonus* and the *motu proprio Apostolos Suos*, among others. *Pastor Bonus* granted greater power to papal primacy and relativized the authority of the Episcopal Conferences. Meanwhile, the curia began to produce its own theology. *Apostolos Suos* limited the teaching function of the bishops to following the universal magisterium as officially interpreted by the Holy See (*AS* 21). To these documents we can add the Instruction of Diocesan Synods, *De Synodis Dioecesanis Agendis*, which dealt a severe blow to the ecclesiology of local churches by prohibiting diocesan synods from pronouncing on any subject "that does not agree with the Church's perpetual doctrine or the papal magisterium" (IDS, IV, no. 4).

The Extraordinary Synod of 1985—the Twentieth Anniversary of the Conclusion of the Second Vatican Council—represented an inflection point that discounted the ecclesiology of the people of God and assumed the model of *hierarchical communion* as central to the interpretation and implementation of the conciliar event. Avery Dulles wrote that "the question before the Extraordinary Synod of 1985 was not—as some commentators imagined—whether to affirm or reject Vatican II, but rather *how to interpret it*"; its intention was that, "guided by a *hermeneutics of unity*, the ecclesiology of the future may be able to correct some of the imbalances of the past two decades."[2] Dulles also pointed out the correlation that existed between this ecclesiological shift and the views of the then prefect of the Congregation for the Doctrine of the Faith, Cardinal Ratzinger.[3] In the following years, consequently, a redefinition of identities and a reconfiguration of relationships among all ecclesial subjects in the Church were implemented through a series of synods that considered the laity (1987), priests (1990), religious life (1994), and bishops (2001). The fruits of the synods were gathered in the postsynodal exhortations *Christifideles Laici* (1988), *Pastores Dabo Vobis* (1992), *Vita Consecrata* (1996), and *Pastores Gregis* (2003).

The way the faithful relate to one another in the Church was reconfigured to conform to the model of the Church as hierarchical communion. According to the resulting notion of coresponsibility, priests, laypeople, and religious interacted with the episcopate only in terms of auxiliary, vertical relations. The notion of coresponsibility was no longer understood as an essential and reciprocal relationship that completes ecclesial identities in their interactions, as Cardinal Suenens had sustained in his interpretation of the Council. Theology, itself, became less autonomous and was subordinated to the magisterium, while formation in the faith was focused on the *Catechism*. Consequently, the teaching and the transmission of the faith was subjected to a process of homogenization.

The 1992 document *Communionis Notio* distanced itself even further from the spirit and the letter of the Council by declaring that the universal Church is an ontological, preexisting reality, thus universalizing the identity of ecclesial life, and reinforcing institutional homogenization according to the Roman theological-cultural pattern.[4] Walter Kasper confronted this position of Joseph Ratzinger by warning that it negated the ecclesiology of communion among local churches, reinforced the centralism of the Roman curia, and eroded the value of the episcopal conferences as intermediate instances. While Ratzinger's aim may have been to safeguard the *communio ecclesiae*, he ended up favoring the *communio hierarchica* and relativizing the sense of *communio ecclesiarum*, with all the newness that this concept brought to the ecclesiology of the Vatican as compared to that of Vatican I.[5]

To resolve this argument, authors like Salvador Pié-Ninot use the term *catholicity* to refer to "the whole or the entire rather than to the totality,"[6] with latter term describing what is universal. As Rahner says, "The local Church makes the entire Church tangible."[7] The *Instrumentum Laboris* of the Synod for the Amazon explained the matter clearly: "To be Church is to be the People of God, incarnated in the peoples of the earth and their cultures. The universality or catholicity of the Church is therefore enriched by the beauty of these multifaceted manifestations of the particular Churches and their cultures" (*IL* 12), all of which make up the *communio ecclesiarum.* Consequently, "the concept of the particular Church would adapt better to the diverse regional realizations of the Church that express its cultural pluralism."[8]

RECOVERING THE "CATHOLICITY" OF LOCAL CHURCHES

Synodality deepens and expands the Second Vatican Council's ecclesiology of the local church and its relations with the catholicity of the whole Church. An example of this is how the *Synod on Synodality* has been conceived: it is not to be understood as merely an isolated *event* but has become a two-year *process* that begins with a diocesan phase exercising the first level of synodality, that of the local churches. As Cardinal Mario Grech, secretary general of the Synod of Bishops, has stated,

> Considering that *the local churches, in which and from which the one and only Catholic Church exists,* contribute effectively to the good of the entire mystical body, which is also the body of the churches (cf. *Lumen Gentium* 23), *the fullness of the synodal process can truly exist only if the local churches are involved in that process.* For a genuine participation of the local churches in this process, there must also be the involvement of other ecclesial bodies, such as the Synods of the Eastern Catholic Churches, the Councils and Assemblies of the Churches *sui iuris*, and the Episcopal Conferences with their own national, regional, and continental entities.[9]

This is a clear reception of *Lumen Gentium*, which recognizes that "in and from [the local] Churches comes into being the one and only Catholic Church" and that "this variety of local Churches with one common aspiration is splendid evidence of the catholicity of the undivided Church" (*LG* 23).[10] Catholicity, therefore, refers to the *fullness* that characterizes the local churches and to the communion that exists among them in virtue of their relation to the Church of Rome and its bishop, the pope. This is how *subsistit in*, the famous phrase in *Lumen Gentium* 8, is to be understood: the Church of Christ—not the Universal Church—*subsists in* the Roman Catholic Church.

Gérard Philips, the principal redactor of *Lumen Gentium*, recognized the centrality of this ecclesiology,[11] according to which the local church, while not the *whole* Church, is a *complete* Church,[12] and he knew the many repercussions it would have on theological and ecclesial issues. Legrand also recognized "what is new about Vatican II: in addition to affirming that the catholicity of the entire Church is nourished by the richness of the different local Churches, Vatican II affirms *the catholicity of the diocesan Church itself*."[13] The great challenge still facing the postconciliar Church is in becoming *a worldwide* Church. For that to happen, argues Rahner, *cultural differences* must become configuring factors of the local churches' catholicity.[14] For this reason, the universal Church exists only in concrete communities that are incarnated in and through their own sociocultural forms.

In the ecclesial model of the New Testament, Brighenti explains that

> the Churches being born do not exist as "Churches *of*," that is, as specific instances of a universal Church that supposedly precedes them. Rather they are "Churches *in*" the same unique Church, which is whole (entire) in each local church. The local church is configured not as a branch or a copy of a supposed *mother Church*,

but as a *different Church*, universal in its particularities, with its own culturally unique features.[15]

Jerusalem, Corinth, Antioch, and Macedonia were all born as local Catholic Churches in different sociocultural places that gave them a special identity and physiognomy. In other words, the local church becomes *real* in the cultural forms in which it exists. Or as Paul VI said, "A Church spread throughout the world would become an abstraction if it did not take on body and life precisely through the individual Churches" (*EN* 62) with all their theological, liturgical, spiritual, pastoral, and canonical particularities (*LG* 23, *UR* 4, *AG* 19).

The call to recover the centrality of the ecclesiology of local churches is perhaps one of the most important contributions of the current phase in the reception of the Council. It is shaping the way in which the institution of the Synod of Bishops is understood and functions as a "dynamic point of convergence" of all local churches. But most importantly, it is providing a new hermeneutical framework for understanding the ecclesiological shift that synodality represents today. It opens a path toward a "more complete definition of the Church" that integrates and interconnects *Lumen Gentium* and *Ad Gentes*, conceiving ecclesiology as a "permanent process of *ecclesiogenesis*."[16]

ECCLESIOLOGY AS *ECCLESIOGENESIS*

To implement the first level of the exercise of synodality, we must move beyond fragmentary interpretations of *Lumen Gentium* and *Ad Gentes*. If we are to follow a synodal way of proceeding, then *ecclesiology* must always be *ecclesiogenesis*. This involves recovering "the perception of Vatican II according to which 'the sociocultural particularity of a region' (*AG* 22) is part of a local Church's *theological definition*"[17] and thus configures the local church's identity and form in accord with its place and time. This is what we have called a *Church of Churches*.[18]

The third chapter of *Ad Gentes* provides a more appropriate hermeneutical framework for ecclesial reconfiguration because it relates the birth of particular churches to their sociocultural areas; in this way, it helps them to develop ecclesial traditions that are not only their own but also contribute to strengthening communion with other churches (*AG* 22). It is in those churches and in their communion that the catholicity of the entire Church is realized. For this reason,

> the *Ad Gentes* decree is probably the one that best shows how the universality of the mission demands that believers take human cultures into account and so establish particular Churches. Since the Church is Catholic, it must become particular in the cultures it encounters... to the point that the local Churches will be truly Catholic only at the end of a process of inculturation.[19]

The ecclesiology of local churches, therefore, presupposes an *inculturation* that is in tune with *Ad Gentes*, which focuses on the *evangelical witness* (*AG* 24) found in communities gathered around the Word (no. 15) and engaged in dialogue with the local reality (nos. 6, 11). From such communities must emerge new expressions of ministry that respond to each theological-cultural reality (nos. 15, 19). *Ad Gentes* is very clear on this last point, advising that

> it is not enough that the Christian people be present and be organized in a given nation, nor is it enough to

carry out an apostolate by way of example....In order to plant the Church and to make the Christian community grow, various ministries are needed, which are raised up by divine calling from the midst of the faithful congregation, and are to be carefully fostered and tended to by all. (no. 15)

By interpreting *LG* and *AG* in a manner that is more comprehensive and process oriented, we can now identify more clearly the incredible newness of the shift brought about by the ecclesiology of Vatican II: it recognized contextual reality as normative for reconfiguring the Church's identity and theological-cultural self-understanding, as well as for guiding its mission in the world.[20] *Gaudium et Spes* clarifies the implications of this shift when it states that the Church "has learned to express the message of Christ with the help of the ideas and terminology of different peoples and has tried to clarify it with their wisdom too" (*GS* 44). Thus, the "cultures or lifestyles"[21] of the peoples are inseparable from their ecclesial forms and their Christian way of life. In other words, the Council recognized that, since culture refers to the "various styles of common life" (no. 53), the Church must "adapt the revealed word" to the many diverse ways of life of the peoples. Such adaptation is necessary because "revelation is completely historical and therefore subject to constant reinterpretation, according to the situation of those to whom it is transmitted."[22]

In this synodal way, the Church "constantly reshapes her identity through listening and through dialogue with the people, the realities, and the history of the lands in which she finds herself" (*QA* 66), discerning "how their customs, their views on life, and their social order can be reconciled with the manner of living taught by divine revelation" (no. 22). Such a process leads to "a more profound adaptation in the whole area of Christian life" (no. 22), which means that "in each major socio-cultural area, such theological speculation should be encouraged, in the light of the universal Church's tradition, as may submit to a new scrutiny the words and deeds which God has revealed, and which have been set down in Sacred Scripture and explained by the Fathers and by the magisterium" (no. 22).

This is the core of what is called the *principle of pastorality*,[23] which requires the Church to perform an act of *reinterpretation* of Christianity for each culture in the light of the Word and tradition, and to engage in a process of theological-cultural reconfiguration of its own forms and institutions (*QA* 68). The interpretation of doctrine (*traditum*) has always been linked to the mode of its reception (*receptio*) according to the logic "*quidquid recipitur ad modum recipientis recipitur*" (see *Summa Theologiae* I, q.75, a.5). Thus, ecclesiality is born of ecclesiogenesis. The lived context of the community is thematized and structured at this first level of synodality. "By this manner of acting...Christian life will be accommodated to the genius and the dispositions of each culture, so that particular traditions, together with the peculiar patrimony of each family of nations, illumined by the light of the Gospel, can be taken up into Catholic unity" (*AG* 22).

This was the approach that, from the third century, inspired diocesan and provincial synods that dealt with issues of discipline, liturgy, and doctrine. The Gregorian Reforms and the Council of Trent produced a shift toward theological-cultural homogeni-zation and centralization of the institutional Church, with the consequent loss of the synodal praxis and consciousness of the diocesan churches. Pope Francis, in line with the Second Vatican Council, is now urging us to recover the path of synodality as an essential constituent dimension of the Church of the third mil-lennium. We should especially consider the ecclesial practice of the first millennium, when "local Churches are communitarian subjects that make the one People of God real in a novel way in different cultural contexts, and they share their gifts in a reciprocal exchange in order to promote 'bonds of close communion.'"[24]

In short, to recover the exercise of synodality at this level is to affirm that "the variety of local Churches—with their own ecclesiastical disciplines, liturgical rites, theological heritage, spiritual gifts, and canonical norms—'is splendid evidence of the catholicity of the undivided Church.'"[25] A synodal ecclesiology acknowledges that catholicity is realized in the model of a Church of Churches because "the synodal dimension of the Church implies communion in the living faith of the various local Churches with each other and with the Church of Rome."[26]

10

The Latin American Church—a Case Study

A synodal ecclesiology has been the principal channel for receiving Vatican II in Latin America. It seeks to guarantee that what is characteristic of each local Church contributes to the growth and the unity of the entire Church (*LG* 13). The post-synodal exhortation *Querida Amazonia* explains this point well when it states, "Everything that the Church has to offer must become incarnate in a distinctive way in each part of the world.... Preaching must become incarnate, spirituality must become incarnate, ecclesial structures must become incarnate" (*QA* 6).[1] Consequently, the Latin American Church is a *source Church* that has been able to reconfigure herself, producing a regional and communal pastoral *style* and creating its own ecclesial *structures*. It does this by enhancing a communion of local churches through joint processes and programs that culminate in Continental *events*—either *collegial*, such as the General Conferences of Bishops, or *synodal*, such as the recently called Ecclesial Assembly of Latin America and the Caribbean. Most importantly, it is a real, concrete example of how the Church can reconfigure herself in a synodal key.

A NEW WAY OF BEING CHURCH

To end our reflection, we offer an example of how synodality can emerge and be lived, even when it has not yet been consciously thematized or theologized. As Gilles Routhier states,

> Synodality cannot be reduced to formal mechanics, as if the establishment of institutional figures and the implementation of the corresponding procedures and practices were enough to assure us life. On the contrary, synodality can also exist where there are no established formal processes. At this infra-institutional level, it depends largely on people's ability to listen and their willingness to learn from others. It depends on those who perform the function of presiding, on their understanding of their ministry, and on their awareness of this function of presiding over the Church of God; this function has been entrusted to the ordained ministers, but it does not separate them from (or empower them over) the other members of the *Ecclesia Dei*. Consequently, synodality, which requires spiritual attitudes, depends to a great extent on the relational skills of those who hold positions of authority and on their ability to relate to others as brothers, friends, collaborators, and cooperators.[2]

Synodality Broadens and Completes Collegiality

When Vatican II began, the Latin American Church already had a collegial structure. The creation of the Latin American Bishops Council (CELAM) in 1955 had resulted in a distinctive working relationship that encouraged a permanent flow of information among the local churches of Latin America and the Caribbean, which were represented by their respective bishops' conferences. CELAM's organizational and consultative character, defined in its first statutes as an "organ for contact and collaboration," allowed for the emergence of an authentically regional approach that broadened and completed a collegial way of proceeding. Using this new structure, Paul VI announced on January 20, 1968, the convening of the Second General Conference of Latin American Bishops and, on August 24, 1968, he inaugurated the event with a speech delivered at the cathedral of Bogotá. The Medellín Conference took place at the seminary in Medellín between August 26 and September 6, 1968.[3]

With the emergence of this collaborative working method among local churches, local clergy gained a greater awareness of their own theological and ecclesial contribution to the Church's life. While it is true that the concept of collegiality was thematized during the Second Vatican Council, it was already being practiced among the Latin American bishops, who "effectively affirmed their bonds of union and their shared consciousness."[4] Cecilio de Lora notes, "Ten years before the Second Vatican Council promulgated the doctrine of episcopal collegiality (*LG* 22), the Latin American Church was practicing it, not with words but with works and in truth: it was something truly prophetic that would later serve as a model for other churches through the universal Church."[5]

This unity between doctrine and pastoral sensibility that had been achieved in Latin America long before the Council allowed for an experience of collegiality that was different from its traditional, juridical form. Since the bishops were truly representing a *portio Populi Dei* and exercising their ministry of pastoral service to the people while situated in this world, their awareness of belonging to a college of bishops could not be understood apart from a real and obligatory relation to the people and their historical circumstances. As noted at the Medellín Conference, a particular part of the people is called to constitute "a particular Church, in which the Church of Christ—one, holy, catholic, and apostolic—is truly found and truly operates" (Final Document, "Pastoral de conjunto," 17). This is a *situated* collegiality, which gets lost when collegiality is understood as deriving from episcopal ordination per se, and when it is thought that bishops can exist without representing a *portio Populi Dei*, that is, as functionaries who do not exercise ministry and so produce doctrine without pastoral sensibility.

As the Medellín documents make clear, episcopal communion does not exist for the self-preservation of the *communio hierarchica*. For this reason, Landázuri Ricketts insisted that "the deepening of our collegiality allows us to discern the meaning of our pastoral action in a Latin American context; it determines our action." He also warned, "But there is something more: the presence of the poor should condition and govern our joint pastoral plans."[6] There is thus a progressive broadening of collegiality that comes from the lived experience of a pastoral approach that makes an unambiguous option for the poor and is based on a "people of God" ecclesiology.

Jorge Mejía summed up what happened in Medellín when he stated that "there was above all an experience of episcopal collegiality, nourished and completed by the experience of the communion of each and every person, which is the Church."[7] It is interesting to observe that he insisted that it is this communion of each and every person that bestows a note of completeness to episcopal collegiality. It is thus possible to speak of the contextual practice of coresponsibility on the part of all Church members for the common good of the people of God because of the pastoral nature of collegial activity. The spirit of coresponsibility should be founded on the common baptismal identity of all the faithful, by which all are responsible for ecclesial communion and mission. This identity is to be experienced in the ecclesial community—not individually or privately—and it is to be experienced horizontally by all those who live the life of the people of God. Therefore, this "spirit" should be "institutionalized." Accordingly, as we read in the Medellín documents, "The lay community, by reason of its common priesthood, enjoys the right and has the duty to collaborate in making an indispensable contribution to pastoral action. It is therefore the duty of the priests to dialogue with them not just occasionally but constantly and in an established manner" (Final Document, "Sacerdotes," 16).

The Latin American adoption and exercise of an "essential" and "reciprocal" coresponsibility, rather than an auxiliary and vertical one, made manifest the unity and communion existing among all the local churches of the continent. At the same time, it affiliated them to the universal Church while preserving their proper regional or continental identity. It was a true *communio ecclesiarum*. This will give us some idea of what José Oscar Beozzo meant by "the exercise of broadened collegiality at Medellín." The novelty of this phenomenon, in his judgment, was visible mainly in *the assembly's working method*, which was not repeated in the same way at any other episcopal conference. The participants at Medellín were able to move beyond a narrow vision of collegiality, which would have reduced the conference to being merely a consultative body for the Roman pontiff. They put into practice "a broadened notion of collegiality, one that bestows responsibility for the life and mission of the Church on the totality of the People of God."[8]

Synodality as Listening and Consulting

CELAM had fostered the contextual practice that moved the bishops toward a shared identity. Before the Medellín Conference, CELAM had held eleven ordinary meetings, one each year. It had twelve departments that provided consulting and formation services to the churches on the continent, and it had four institutes dedicated to research in different cities. Moreover, between 1966 and 1968, it had convened six specialized meetings for planning the doctrinal orientation of the Medellín Conference.

While journeying on this road to Medellín, the bishops experienced true ecclesiality and developed an ecclesial style that involved working together in groups and adopting collegial forms of action. "By using these methods people came together to communicate their experiences and to analyze their concerns; in this way new life was generated, and they began to see the big picture. One has to remember the isolation that had previously prevailed and the lack of opportunities for meeting together."[9] This ecclesial style was unprecedented, because never before had there been sociocultural and ecclesial interaction of such magnitude. It was also different from traditional collegial practice, where every form of exchange in the Church was determined primarily by juridical logic and an ontological metaphysics. A decisive step was thus taken from an ecclesiastical style that was monocultural, juridical, and Roman to one that was multicultural, charismatic, and regional. The shift necessitated a search for ways in which to integrate local differences and create a greater unity in fidelity to the conciliar spirit.

The Council had developed the theme of collegiality (*LG* 22–23) but not that of synodality, which was often identified with the collegial activity of the bishops in conciliar meetings. Consequently, synodality lost its broader meaning and its application to the different levels in which it could be exercised by the people of God: among bishops (*affectus collegialis*); between bishops and priests (*communio sacramentalis* in the ministerial priesthood); and in relation to laypeople (coresponsibility). A significant difficulty (one that persists) was a certain failure to broaden synodality to include consultation with all the faithful rather than limiting it to the two traditional, institutional forms—councils and synods.

At Medellín, the living out of ecclesial communion in fraternal and filial solidarity was accompanied by a mode of interacting in which it was neither juridical authority nor majority vote that guaranteed concurrence with respect to judgments made and decisions taken; it was rather "the phenomenon of the bishops' convergence among themselves."[10] This is what Landázuri Ricketts called the "convergence of prophetic circumstances,"[11] a convergence that gave rise to positive personal and sociocultural attitudes and actions, such as listening and consulting rather than just cold analysis of historical conditions. The process of listening and consulting gave direction and meaning to the decisions taken by the bishops at Medellín. Those decisions were based on concern for the common good of the people and designed to shape pastoral practice in accord with the historical reality of the poor.

In its implementation of the spirit of the Council, Medellín effectively articulated the *sensus fidelium* of all the faithful and the *munus docendi* of the hierarchy. This made it possible for those attending to participate in decision-making and to exercise the Church's prophetic dimension. What was achieved was a *singularis antistitum et fidelium conspiratio* (*Dei Verbum* 10), that is, a singular synergy among all the members of the assembly through dialogue and discernment, leading to collaborative redaction of the assembly's conclusions. This *conspiratio* shaped the way in which synodality was articulated by the conference—and this apart from determining whether there was any exercise of core-sponsibility, any delegation of consultative function, or any clarity as to whom had the right to vote. In other words, the synodal spirit manifested at Medellín presupposed a model of Church as people of God that gave primacy to the *sensus fidei* and to the *sensus fidelium* (LG 12). Thus, the infallibility *in credendo* of the whole people of God—experienced in a concrete historical reality—was the context within which the pastors' infallibility *in docendo* was exercised.

We can add that the Medellín Conference inaugurated a new way of being Church, presenting a programmatic vision defined by a synodal spirit and style and allowing for the exercise of collegiality in a contextual, unthematized manner. This synodal spirit, by encouraging the "experience of the communion of one and all which is the Church," led to the embrace of "unity amid differences."[12] As José Beozzo noted, "No other continent had an event comparable to Medellín, which was an exemplary case of a continental and collegial reception of Vatican II. It was carried out faithfully but at the same time selectively and creatively with respect to the principal inspirations of the Council."[13]

The first person to acknowledge explicitly that something new was transpiring was Cardinal Landázuri Ricketts, who, in his closing discourse, stated,

> The word "collegiality," if we fully accede to its theological and pastoral demands, can help us make our arguments more effectively. During these days we have witnessed something audacious, though its import is still unclear: Latin America has begun to have a dynamic of its own. Our collegiality is defined by this fact....We have received the Spirit the Lord promised us, and in that Spirit our collegiality is a fact and an

event. Therefore, what the experience of these days tells us is that this *Second General Conference*, with its new spirit and style, will begin when it concludes. The conference is a starting point that has given us a deeper awareness of what we are. Collegiality does not require physical proximity. Therefore, our experience of these days gives us a firm hope that we will continue living this unity in plurality.[14]

In his judgment, collegiality was not something graded or hierarchical but rather something that functioned in terms of its own internal and relational dynamic. Consequently, he could affirm that "it does not require physical proximity" but is rather consummated in relations and attitudes. "Our experience of these days gives us a firm hope that we will continue living this unity in plurality. Prayer, reflection, dialogue, mutual concern—these are the attitudes that have characterized our sessions, and they should remain in our hearts now that we are returning to our local churches."[15]

In sum, in Medellín there was an attitude of mutual listening and fraternal acceptance that was able to unleash a collective process—de facto or de jure—of discernment and of convergence among persons. Mejía's testimony moves in this direction:

Here we live and work and pray for fifteen days, until September 7th. The three hundred people ... attending the conference fraternize at table, at liturgical celebrations, and in discussions. Such leveling of cardinals, archbishops, vowed religious, and laymen and laywomen is already real progress and a good sign for the future. No church conference could have done this five years ago. And I confess that nobody seems to be uncomfortable. The liturgy makes a contribution, for that is its proper role and its efficacy. Most priests concelebrate (not all, unfortunately), which means that all of a sudden more than two hundred concelebrants leave the triple sacristy in procession to take their places in the elegant oval of the church, with the altar at one end. A layperson reads the epistle. There is a lot of fine singing. Communion is given under both species. The new canons are used. The kiss of peace is shared among all. We really pray, and we are transformed.[16]

The conference highlighted these relational and practical dimensions, and it stressed procedures that would foster the strong bonds that give meaning to the Christian experience, the purpose always being "to reach all sectors of the People of God and create a single ecclesial consciousness in bishops, priests, religious, laypeople, and all movements and associations" (Final Document, "Pastoral de conjunto," 35). The assembly went so far as to criticize church structures that it considered out of tune with the Council's orientation, and it did so in language that reflected the need to give new life to a synodal way of proceeding:

Among the realities we view negatively are the following: (a) the inadequacy of the traditional structures of many parishes in providing a true community experience; (b) a quite generalized impression that diocesan curias are administrative bureaucracies; (c) the distress of many priests at not finding decisive solutions to some priestly crises, and also, by analogy, to the crises of a large number of religious and laypeople; (d) individualistic attitudes in persons and institutions in situations that require good coordination; (e) cases where collaborative ministry or planning has been poorly practiced, the reasons for which may be sheer improvisation, technical incompetence, excessive valuation of "plans," or an excessively rigid and authoritarian conception of their place in pastoral practice. (Final Document, "Pastoral de conjunto," 4)

Synodality as Discernment and Dialogue

For Beozzo, the novelty of this practice was "etched in the *working methods* adopted at Medellín and also partly in the votes that were taken."[17] Besides adapting the tone and the method of *Gaudium et Spes*, the Medellín Conference took place in an environment of discernment that fostered an attitude of listening and dialogue in small groups and plenary sessions. The initial deliberations that took place led to focusing on sixteen key areas, the study and discussion of which would culminate in the sixteen documents that formed the Final Document. McGrath recalled that "it [had been] decided not to arrive at the conference with a pre-existing text to which only amendments would be made. The method we followed was very different. The first few days would be dedicated to listening and followed by discussions in small groups and plenary sessions."[18]

The participants at the assembly were confident of their ability to create something new through the style of work they had set in place. Since they were not starting out with a predetermined method that was to be applied, it was possible to require the approval of everyone attending the assembly, not just the bishops. This was the case even though the participants were theoretically divided into voting members and simple participants (those without the right to vote).[19] The work of reflection and redaction was done in the commissions and in small teams; the texts were then discussed by all in the plenaries,[20] which were attended "not only by the bishops but by many priests, religious, and laity, thus opening up a new style of collaboration in the Church's work."[21]

This dynamic gave rise to a genuine *conspiratio*, which was possible because of *a disposition to listen and learn*, the basis of every form of synodal action. It is in virtue of this act of listening that Medellín reaffirmed the principle of the Church's continual reformation (*Unitatis Redintegratio* 6), stating that "all revision of church structures, to the extent that they can be reformed, should be done to satisfy the demands of concrete historical situations, but also with an eye to the church's nature. The revision should be carried out in view of the present situation of our continent, and it should be inspired and oriented by the two guiding principles that were greatly stressed in the Council: communion and catholicity (*Lumen Gentium* 13)" (Final Document, "Pastoral de conjunto," 5).

The need to reexamine Church and social structures derived not from the Church's reflection on itself but from its reflection on its mission in the Latin American and Caribbean world. Therefore, the reflection was far removed from any self-referential and clericalist perspective, and it recognized that "for an analysis of this type it is necessary to listen more to experts and laypeople" (Final Document, "Pastoral de las élites," 4). This required that laypeople be members of commissions, functioning not as simple advisors to clerics but as autonomous and authoritative contributors who offer their reflections on the subjects pertinent to each commission, according to their expertise.

In this spirit of horizontal listening, the first thing participants in the assembly at Medellín did was open their ears to a series of concrete facts about the Latin American reality that were not well known in traditional ecclesial circles. This helped form the strong social sensibility and clear pastoral orientation that would characterize all the group discussions at the conference, as well as the documents that resulted from it. Bishop Samuel Ruiz recalled that Medellín's reception of the Council involved "changing the conception and attitude by which we place the Church outside the world and against it. The Church is the People of God engaged in making history; the Church is in the world."[22] Accordingly, the foremost disposition proposed by the bishops was listening so as to serve. "We want to show sincere respect for all men and women, and we want to listen to them in order to help them with their problems and their anxieties" (Final Document, "Pobreza de la Iglesia," 18). This act of listening took place while recognizing and honoring the *sensus fidei* of the people of God, for it was the same God who was communicating himself through them. The collegial response consists of interpreting what has been heard while paying special attention to the cry of the poor. The bishops at Medellín repeated the words that Paul VI addressed to the poor farmers of Colombia: "We hear the cry that rises up from your suffering" (Final Document, "Pobreza de la Iglesia," 2).

In the synodal practice of collegiality, two dimensions of listening stand out: the discernment and interpretation proper to the episcopal college assembled, and the *conspiratio* of all members of the people of God. In other words, there is an effort to maintain the conciliar dynamic among the one (the pope), the many (the bishops), and all (the people). Such an effort is possible when there is a desire to reconcile divergent positions by means of a *conspiratio* that achieves forms of ecclesial consensus, which in turn become the convictions requisite for the life of the Church. Such a vision incorporates the reception of *Dei Verbum* with its assertion that the Word of God has been entrusted to "the whole People of God, united to their pastors," who together "constitute a singular consensus" (*fidelium conspiratio*) and thus establish an essential and reciprocal relation between *sensus fidei* and magisterium (see *DV* 10).

Only this situated kerygmatic configuration, based on hearing the word in the history of the people, allows for the translation of the message into the actual forms in which it is received. This is truly an application of the conciliar principle of the pastorality of doctrine, which "requires unceasing labor so that the message of salvation contained in the scriptures, the liturgy, the magisterium, and the testimony is perceived today as the word of life. There is a constant need to express the 'Gospel' in ever new ways, in relation to human forms of existence, taking into account ethical and cultural conditions and remaining always faithful to the revealed Word" (Final Document, "Catequesis," 15).

To achieve this, therefore, the Conference understood that authentic ecclesial reform was not to be reduced to simple change of structures or of persons running the structures; rather, it would concentrate on ways of assisting the flow of communication among the structures and among those operating within them, and thus facilitate the synodal way of working:

> It is therefore essential that all the ecclesial communities remain open to the dimension of Catholic communion so that none becomes closed in on itself. This is a task particularly incumbent on the hierarchical ministers, especially on the bishops, who, collegially united with their head, the Roman Pontiff, are the principle of the catholicity of the churches. In order for such openness to be effective and not purely juridical, there must be genuine communication, upward and downward, between the base and the summit. (Final Document, "Pastoral de conjunto," 8)

Synodality as Unity and Diversity

Synodal forms of ecclesiality or true articulation of collegiality are developed from within-outward and from below-upward (from base communities and parishes to hierarchical-charismatic structuring). In the words with which Landázuri Ricketts inaugurated the conference, "During these days of labor, let us be very attentive to the Christian stance—for it is Christ's—of taking the world as it is, from below. Only in this way will we follow the incarnational road that Jesus has begun."[23] Accordingly, the assembly's reflection was always oriented toward "unity in mission and diversity in charisms, services, and functions" (Final Document, "La iglesia visible," 7–8; and "Sacerdotes," 7), to allow for differentiated participation of the people of God. The distinction being made was not hierarchical, but rather, was a horizontal and reciprocal differentiation of members by reason of the "threefold prophetic, priestly, and kingly function of Christ" incumbent on every baptized person (Final Document, "La iglesia visible," 8). This foundation made possible an "organic and articulated" way of proceeding (Final Document, "Pastoral de conjunto," 9) that enabled each member to contribute something to the other members according to his or her specific function and place in the Church and society. Thus, there was, for example, discussion of what was most proper to "the layperson's commitment to liberation and humanization in the world" (Final Document, "La iglesia visible," 9, 13).

The conciliar spirit of *Lumen Gentium* was deepened at Medellín through the support for attitudes conducive to thinking, discerning, and planning as a body. The Council had affirmed the value of this type of genuine, organic communication, which moves from the base upward:

The laity are, by reason of the knowledge, competence, or outstanding ability which they may enjoy, permitted and sometimes even obliged to express their opinion on those things which concern the good of the Church....Let the spiritual shepherds recognize and promote the dignity as well as the responsibility of the laity in the Church. Let them willingly employ their prudent advice. Let them confidently assign duties to them in the service of the Church, allowing them freedom and room for action.

The Conference saw this model exemplified in a new structure, the small Christian base communities: they are "the first and fundamental ecclesial nucleus, and they should, at their own level, take responsibility for enriching and spreading of the faith, as well as for fostering the worship which is its expression." These communities are the "embryonic cells of ecclesial structuring and evangelizing, and actually a primary force for human flourishing and development" (Final Document, "Pastoral de conjunto," 10).

The reason for promoting base communities is that they allow for the exercise of the fraternal spirit of synodality, something not found nowadays in the structure of parishes based on territory rather than on homogeneous communities. "Christians should be able to experience the communion to which they have been called in their base communities, that is, in local or regional communities that correspond to the reality of homogeneous groups and that allow for personal and fraternal relationships among their members" (Final Document, "Pastoral de conjunto," 10).

The new ecclesial context envisions the parish, within the framework of the synodal spirit, as a "vivifying and unifying pastoral ensemble of base communities" (Final Document, "Pastoral de conjunto," 13). The parish acts to facilitate the interaction among the communities that belong to it; it is not an end in itself, a closed space, but rather a community of communities. In other words, it is analogous to the universal Church, which is one institution amid others in society and contributes to local development. Such a view adds clarity to the affirmation above regarding Christians experiencing communion in base communities, which enable the formation of personal and fraternal relationships among members ("Pastoral de conjunto," 10). More importantly, "the community will be formed to the extent that its members have a sense of belonging, a sense of being 'we'" (Final Document, "Pastoral popular," 13). This "we" will enable true upward and downward communication, properly aligned with the dynamics of belonging and reciprocity that it creates, through the collaboration and representation of the "People of God in the diversity of their conditions and states of life" (Final Document, "Pastoral de conjunto," 18). This path not only leads to authentic declericalization and decentralization of the Church, it rescues its properly missionary dimension and promotes coparticipation in its governance (Final Document, "Pastoral de conjunto," 19).

In conclusion, this concrete case study of synodal ecclesiality through the Medellín Conference signified a reception of the Council that allowed the Latin American Church to position itself as a *source Church*, a Church that had not only created, with the formation of CELAM, a collegial form of continental interaction but had also inaugurated a spirit of being and working and a mode of interaction that gave rise to a synodal way of proceeding as part of its identity. The reception of the Council's ecclesiology of the people of God and the ecclesiology of local churches have been key to understanding the emergence of a practice and style that give identity and form to a way of being Church.

NEW SPIRIT, NEW STRUCTURES

The Creation and Restructuring of CELAM

As noted, the *structure* of CELAM favored a new ecclesial organizational model and fostered greater pastoral cooperation among the local bishops' conferences. With its continental reach, it is an unprecedented ecclesial formation which, "for the first time in the history of the *conventus episcoporum*, finds institutional expression."[24] The novelty of CELAM is that it arises from an ecclesiology of local churches that recognizes the theological status of the region's sociocultural reality and reconfigures the Church's ways of being and living accordingly. Consequently, each particular church is wedded into greater communion with other churches in the region and into the entire people of God and the universal Church.

In 2018, CELAM began a process of synodal restructuring[25] that was carried out with the participation not only of the continent's bishops but also of other ecclesial subjects—laity, religious, priests—and other ecclesiastical institutions, such as Caritas, the Confederation of Latin American Religious (CLAR), the Latin American and Caribbean Migration Network, Shelter and Human Trafficking (CLAMOR), the Pan-Amazonian Ecclesial Network (REPAM), and so on. Private consulting and auditing firms also took part.[26] For three years the bishops listened, discerned, and received advice. At the end of the process, a new administrative model was approved, reforming, thus, "the organizational framework" in its "three complementary components: *structures* (areas, functions, and reporting channels); *decisions* (bodies where decisions are articulated and made); and *organizational culture*."[27]

Both the institutional reform and the transformed vision were based on the principles of participation, coresponsibility, and subsidiarity, among others.[28] However, the most novel feature of the process has perhaps been the *decentralized* manner in which decisions were discerned and made. A way of proceeding was implemented that involved diverse instances of shared discernment and deliberation, and everything was done from below upward, culminating in decisions made by episcopal authorities that had participated in all stages of the process.[29] A truly synodal collegial structure will require a new organizational culture based on collaborative work, shared responsibilities, constant dialogue, and the active participation of laypeople, especially women, to overcome longstanding authoritarianism and clericalism.[30]

The Venezuelan Plenary Council

Another recent instance of synodality was the Venezuelan Plenary Council, which sought to understand the documents of the Second Vatican Council in light of the Venezuelan reality.[31] First convened on January 10, 1998, the Plenary Council went through three phases: the prepreparatory phase of informing and motivating (1996–98); the preparatory phase of analyzing the most important issues for the Church in Venezuela (1998–2000); and the meeting phase, which consisted of six annual sessions (2000–2005). Represented at the sessions were all instances and sectors of the Church and society; only 20 percent of those attending were bishops. The Council had its last session on October 7, 2006.

The Plenary Council's methodology included a process of ongoing consultation that took the form of a series of surveys of different sectors of society. The survey responses were processed by the Center for Socio-religious Research (CISOR). For the Council's internal work, sixteen subcommissions were created, in accord with the sixteen documents of Vatican II. All the subcommissions presented consultation schemas, which were used to prepare the preparatory document that formed the basis of discussion in parish, diocesan, and provincial assemblies.

As required by the code of canon law, the bishops had the deliberative vote, but it was decided that the documents of the Plenary Council would be submitted to the consultative vote of all, including the bishops. After this vote was made known to everyone, an initial discussion took place in the council hall, and then the working groups met. Each document was then submitted to the Plenary Council for final approval. When necessary, a document was sent back to the respective subcommission for revision. At the end of each session, each document was voted on by parts in the manner specified in the regulations. A first consultative vote was taken involving everybody, and then the bishops cast the deliberative vote after considering the views of the groups and the whole assembly. The bishops were able to do this because they had themselves participated as simple faithful in the whole process of discerning about decisions to be made and not only in making the final decisions.

National Pastoral Institute

One of the most novel decisions was to create and implement new local structures, such as the National Pastoral Institute (INPAS), which not only imparts formation but also organizes frequent National Pastoral Assemblies, preceded by assemblies at the parish, diocesan, and provincial levels. Currently, this new Institute is working on the reform of the parishes.

National Pastoral Advisory Board

A second structure created was the National Pastoral Advisory Board that designs policies and strategies for joint pastoral action; it is made up of members of different instances and sectors of Church and society, within a coresponsible organizational way of proceeding involving all ecclesial subjects in the pastoral decision-making and decision-taking processes affecting the whole Venezuelan Church.

Ecclesial Conference of the Amazon (CEAMA)

Finally, a third instance of ecclesial synodality was the creation of the Ecclesial Conference of the Amazon (CEAMA), which was officially established on June 29, 2020.[32] The aim of the Conference is to articulate and implement "joint pastoral action with differentiated priorities" (*QA* 97) that are suited to the realities of the local churches of the Amazon region (*QA* 82). The creation of the Conference is a response to the call made by the Amazon synodal process[33] to "create a Pan-Amazonian ecclesial communications network that encompasses the various means used by the particular churches and other ecclesial bodies" (*IL* 129; *DF* 61; *QA* 97; *Aparecida* 479).[34]

The new synodal form proposed by CEAMA can be seen in its choice of a name. It is not a bishops' conference but an ecclesial conference because it integrates ecclesial and nonecclesial subjects at different levels of participation in joint processes of discernment and decision-making. The profile of this structure thus reveals how a renewed model of collegiality is emerging in the light of synodality, for while it is a body attached to the presidency of the CELAM, its membership is mixed and not composed only of bishops. Its participants include the seven bishops' conferences of the Amazonian countries; organizations such as Caritas, CLAR, and REPAM; representatives of indigenous peoples; and experts appointed by the presidency of the CEAMA and by the pope.

SYNODALITY

The CEAMA's power-sharing system of ecclesial and episcopal cogovernance involves diverse subjects in "implementing and directing processes of participation and discernment that are capable of manifesting the dynamic of communion that inspires all ecclesial decisions" (ITC, *Syn* 76). All subjects participate in discussions about prospective decisions that are made by the bishops based on joint discernment and consultation. The three new structures discussed in this final section represent well the decisive emergence of a synodal Church.

Conclusion

"A More Complete Definition of the Church"

As we build a new ecclesial model for the third millennium, Pope Paul VI's words still hold true for explaining the transition the Church must go through. In 1969, he warned,

> In the formation of the new ecclesial mentality... there are those who expect that, as the Church progresses in awareness of herself, there will be a dissolution of the juridical relations and bonds that constitute her as the mystical, visible and organic body of Christ in the historical reality of the world; and there are those who consider this doctrinal process to be a transfer of powers whereby the Church fulfills its mission, to the benefit of the lower degrees compared to the higher ones in the People of God. For our part, we view the Church rather as a deep and organic solidarity.[1]

Today, this organic body of the Church bears the wounds of a fractured institutional model suffering from clericalism. As the Latin American ecclesiologist Ronaldo Muñoz said in 1972, "The *clerical institution* is one of the great *structural obstacles* to discovering the Gospel."[2]

In this sense, the transition toward a new model for the third millennium needs to recognize, first, that we are facing a systemic and structural problem that reveals the weakness of the dominant theological-cultural model, which has become outdated and needs not only renewal but also reform.[3] Amid the polarization resulting from inadequate reception of the Second Vatican Council, we need to remember that "the Church, as the People of God, reveals and gives substance to her being as communion when all her members *journey together*, gather in assembly, and take an active part in her evangelizing mission."[4] Thus, to advance in the reception of the Second Vatican Council, there must be a *synodal reconfiguring* of the ecclesiastical institution, and it must start from the hermeneutical primacy of chapter 2 of *Lumen Gentium* ("On the People of God"), which recognizes the binding and permanent character of the *sensus fidei fidelium* in creating the *consensus omnium fidelium*.

Synodality is more than a synod or a council. Apart from questions about participating in synods or renewing the exercise of collegiality, the challenge is to *synodalize* the whole Church and create new structures for this process. Consequently, there is an urgent need to reform the identity and vocation of the ordained ministry so that laypeople are recognized as *subjects* in virtue of the "radical equality of all through baptism."[5] Such an opening would allow for new relational and communicative dynamics that would help to overcome clericalism. They would also facilitate the processes of listening, discerning, and joint decision-making that express the *sensus ecclesiae totius populi*. Such an advance toward *synodal ecclesiality* requires both a reconfiguration of the identity and interaction of ecclesial subjects within the people of God and a further deepening of episcopal collegiality. Thus, it is necessary to "reform relations and institutions."[6]

In this process, the experience of the base ecclesial communities are very instructive because they have shown that communal discernment "from below" is an effective way to link the processes of *decision-making* and *decision-taking*.[7] For, although synodality takes shape in our walking and meeting and sharing together, it reaches completion only when we discern and make decisions together. As we have seen, synodality "needs to be institutionally translated into places, instances, and organs in which it can be practiced,"[8] and it should express "the circular relationship between the ministry of pastors, the participation and coresponsibility of lay people, and the stimulus coming from the charismatic gifts according to the dynamic circular link between 'one,' 'some,' and 'all'" (ITC, *Syn* 106).

Another illustrative experience can be found in the episcopal ministry of Saint Cyprian, bishop of Carthage, who in the third century proposed that there be "collaborative consultation of bishops, priests, deacons, confessors, and also a substantial number of laity... because no decree can be established that is not ratified by consent of a plurality."[9] If all the faithful take part in the elaboration of decisions, then the decisions made will be an expression of the counsels that the community has given, by exercising its essential pastoral coresponsibility. Moreover, the decisions will be accepted and ratified by the bishop not as his own opinion but as the *sensus totius ecclesiae*, of which he is the authorized representative. As Severino Dianich maintains, "No form of valid, authentic authority is conceivable outside of the ecclesial consensus."[10] We have also seen the value of the model proposed by the Latin American bishops in their successive meetings, from 1968 in

Medellín to Aparecida in 2007. They sought convergences and proposed an ecclesial reconfiguration based on an ecclesiology of small communities.[11]

In this sense, the practice and implementation of synodal ecclesiality will have the task of imagining a Church for the third millennium that is, in the words of the Italian theologian Serena Noceti, "open to facilitating complex processes of community discernment involving parishes, priests, the faithful, and theologians."[12] The Church needs, therefore, *a new ecclesial way of proceeding* in which, according to the Belgian canonist Borras, "the consultative organs elaborate the decision, the final responsibility for which falls to the pastoral authority that assumes it,"[13] thus excluding authorities that have not participated in the processes.[14]

With this objective, the document *Synodality in the Life and Mission of the Church*, published by the International Theological Commission, has clearly stated that "the synodal dimension of the Church must be brought out by enacting and directing discernment processes which bear witness to the dynamism of communion that inspires all ecclesial decisions" (ITC *Syn* 76), because "what affects all must be discussed and approved by all."[15] Thus, making a commitment to "greater synodality requires correct application of canonical dispositions, proper understanding of decision-making modalities, and profound confidence in the People of God—all of which must be linked to the elaboration of the decisions that the pastors must make in order to realize 'the missionary aspiration of reaching everyone' (*EG* 31)."[16]

As we have seen, all this presupposes, among other things, a richer theology of the source and exercise of *potestas* in the Church and its relationship with governance.[17] This is perhaps one of our greatest challenges, but it is important for overcoming clericalism and enabling a new ecclesial culture characterized by dialogue, mutual listening, consulting, consensus building, and accountability at all levels. We must not lose this privileged moment for carrying out a synodal reconfiguration of the Church involving "spiritual, pastoral, and institutional reforms" (*Aparecida* 367). Such synodal reconfiguration of the Church is necessary for the conversion of an institution that has been exceedingly self-referential; the Church, by moving away from its own center, will represent more fully the people who mediate the voice of Christ.

Once more, the normativity of the ecclesiology of the people of God is essential. Following *Lumen Gentium* 12, the document *Episcopalis Communio* reminds us that it is the *totality of the faithful* that can "show universal agreement in matters of faith and morals"; that totality includes all who make up the people of God, "from bishops to the last of the lay faithful" (*EC* 5). The task of the hierarchy, therefore, is to create the "concrete mediations" that are necessary for involving all the faithful. A good example is the request made by the Latin American bishops that even "the laity participate in *the discernment, the decision taking, the planning, and the execution*" of ecclesial matters (*Aparecida* 371). This point was also made by Pope Francis regarding the participation of women in the Church, when he stated, "Since lay men and women are protagonists in the Church...we must promote the integration of women in places where *important decisions are taken*,"[18] and not only where decisions are made or elaborated.

Congar helps us to understand how difficult it is to advance further in considering the laity as full subjects and not mere objects in the Church. He wrote,

> We are still far from understanding the consequences of discovering...that the entire Church is a single People of God and that it is made up of the faithful along with the clergy. We still implicitly have the idea that the Church is formed by the clergy and that the faithful are

> only their beneficiaries or clientele. This frightful con-
> ception has been inscribed in so many structures and
> customs that it seems almost natural and immutable.
> This is a betrayal of the truth. Much still remains to be
> done to declericalize our conception of the Church.[19]

Today, we can say that this understanding will come about only by means of personal conversions and structural reforms inspired by the new ecclesial hermeneutics of respectivity and reciprocity among all ecclesial subjects. Synodality expresses a *new way of proceeding* that "has its point of departure but also its point of arrival in the *People of God*" (*Episcopalis Communio* 7). In other words, "synodality is a constitutive dimension of the Church, and through synodality the Church reveals and *configures herself as the pilgrim People of God*."[20]

In view of this exposition, we can safely affirm that reforming a failed institutional model[21] requires generating a new process of ecclesiogenesis,[22] a process that requires in turn authentic theological-pastoral conversion, re-creation, and reeducation or relearning. It is necessary to touch the very heart of ecclesiology and not just reorganize structures superficially. As we have noted, a renewed Church, as opposed to a new Church, involves not only creative reception of the Council but also theological-cultural re-creation of the foundational spirit that led to the Church's original formation. It is necessary to renew the identities and *good practices* of institutions and the mentalities of ecclesial subjects in order to create the new structures and interactions needed for a synodal Church whose "internal institutions must become more fraternal, more participatory, more open to dialogue, more flexible, and more poor."[23]

Such an ecclesiogenesis leads us to think beyond what now exists so that we allow the Spirit to move us into a *new creative phase* of receiving and implementing the Second Vatican Council. For, as Congar reminds us,

> we must ask ourselves whether *aggiornamento* is enough or whether something else will not be necessary. The question becomes urgent to the extent that the Church's institutions are rooted in a cultural world that no longer has a place in the new cultural world. Our epoch requires a revision of "traditional" forms that goes beyond the plans for adaptation or *aggiornamento*; it requires a new creation. It is not enough simply to maintain and adapt what has existed until now; it is necessary to create something new. Christianity is essential transmission, *traditio*. The only things that can be reinvented are the forms of what has been received. To make the transmission—the *paradosis*—effective and authentic, we must revise and renew the forms that served well for transmission in other times but that now prove to be obstacles to genuine transmission.[24]

Let us finish as we began, that is, by evoking the words of Pope Paul VI in his opening speech at the second session of the Second Vatican Council on September 29, 1963. There, he gave voice to the "desire, the need, and the duty of the Church finally to provide a more *complete definition of itself*."[25] In this new phase of the Council's reception that began with the pontificate of Francis, we are faced with the challenge of building a synodal ecclesiality for the third millennium by advancing in the hermeneutics and the reception of the Church as people of God. Only in this way will we fulfill Pope Paul VI's call for "a more complete definition of the Church." That is what synodality represents today.

Notes

FOREWORD

1. Walter Kasper, "Katholische Kirche," *Staatslexikon* 3 (1987): 325–35 at 330.

2. See Code of Canon Law 1983, Canon 375.

3. See *Das Statut der Gemeinsamen Synode der Bistümer in der Bundesrepublik Deutschland*, Offizielle Gesamtausgabe 1 (Freiburg im Breisgau: Beschlüsse der Vollversammlung, 1976), 856–61. See nos. 2, 13.

CHAPTER 1

1. Ronaldo Muñoz, *Nueva conciencia de la Iglesia en América Latina* (Salamanca: Sígueme, 1974), 362.

2. Yves Congar, *True and False Reform in the Church* (Collegeville, MN: Liturgical Press, 1950/2011), 160.

3. Congar, *True and False Reform*, 153–54.

4. Muñoz, *Nueva conciencia de la Iglesia*, 361.

5. Muñoz, *Nueva conciencia de la Iglesia*, 353.

6. Cf. Severino Dianich and Serena Noceti, *Trattato sulla Chiesa* (Brescia: Queriniana, 2002), 211–12.

7. Royal Commission into Institutional Responses to Child Sexual Abuse, "Religious Institutions," in *Final Report*, vol. 16, bk. 2 (Canberra: Commonwealth of Australia 2017), 616, https://www.childabuseroyalcommission.gov.au/final-report.

8. Cf. "Sexueller Missbrauch an Minderjährigen durch katholische Priester, Diakone und männliche Ordensangehörige im Bereich der Deutschen Bischofskonferenz," Mannheim-Heidelberg-Giessen, September 2018, https://bistumlimburg.de/fileadmin/redaktion/Bereiche/missbrauch/MHG-Studie-gesamt.pdf.

9. Royal Commission, "Religious Institutions," 611–12.

10. Royal Commission, "Religious Institutions," 613.

11. Pope Francis, "The Sovereignty of the People of God: Meeting of the Pope with the Jesuits of Mozambique and Madagascar," La Civilta Cattolica, September 5, 2019, https://www.laciviltacattolica.com/the-sovereignty-of-the-people-of-god-the-pontiff-meets-the-jesuits-of-mozambique-and-madagascar/.

12. Pope Francis, "Opening of the XV Ordinary General Assembly of the Synod of Bishops: Address at the Opening of the Synod of Bishops on Young People, the Faith and Vocational Discernment," October 3, 2018, https://www.vatican.va/content/francesco/en/speeches/2018/october/documents/papa-francesco_20181003_apertura-sinodo.html.

13. Royal Commission, "Religious Institutions," 611.

14. Pope Francis, "Discourse to the Curia: Christmas Greetings for the Roman Curia," December 22, 2014, https://www.vatican.va/content/francesco/en/speeches/2014/december/documents/papa-francesco_20141222_curia-romana.html.

15. Interview given by Pope Francis to Antonio Spadaro, SJ, "Clericalism—That Desire to Lord It over Lay People—Signifies an Erroneous and Destructive Separation of the Clergy, a Type of Narcissism," L'Osservatore Romano, weekly Spanish edition, Year XLV, no. 39 (2,333), September 27, 2013.

16. Pope Francis, "The Sovereignty of the People of God."

17. The report adds that "sexual abuse is an extreme consequence of that dominating attitude." See "Sexueller Missbrauch an Minderjährigen durch katholische Priester," 13.

18. Cf. Royal Commission, "Religious Institutions," 614.

Notes

19. Ángela Rinaldi, "Abuso sexual de menores y corrupción estructural," in *Tolerancia Cero*, ed. Daniel Portillo (México-Madrid: CEPROME-PPC, 2019), 33.

20. Royal Commission, "Religious Institutions," 613.

21. Royal Commission, "Religious Institutions," 614.

22. Royal Commission, "Religious Institutions," 585.

23. Cf. "The Causes and Context of Sexual Abuse of Minors by the Catholic Church in the United States between 1950–2010," 87.91.92. Study by John Jay College of Criminal Justice of City University of New York at the request of the U.S. Catholic Bishops' Conference, 2002, https://www.lib.latrobe.edu.au/research/ageofinquiry/biogs/E000235b.htm.

24. Royal Commission, "Religious Institutions," 641.

25. Jörg Fegert, Michael Kölch, Elisa König, et al., eds., *Schutz vor sexueller Gewalt und Übergriffen in Institutionen* (Ulm: Springer, Universitäts Klinkum, 2018), 305, 309.

26. "Sexueller Missbrauch an Minderjährigen durch katholische Priester," 68.

27. Royal Commission, "Religious Institutions," 586.

28. Royal Commission, "Religious Institutions," 618.

29. "This ecclesiology gives rise to a dual model of Church in which the Church of the clergy is superior and more 'holy' when compared with the Church of the laity." Royal Commission, "Religious Institutions," 620.

30. "The socialization, the identification, the putting into words, the symbolic anticipation becomes something truly important only in the fabric of human existence through the mediation of the structures of acceptance, which are those relational elements that allow for the establishment, in and from the present, of creative linkage with the past for the sake of imagining and configuring the future." Lluís Duch, *Educación y crisis de la modernidad* (Barcelona: Paidós, 1997), 27.

31. Muñoz, *Nueva conciencia de la Iglesia*, 362–63.

CHAPTER 2

1. Cf. Pope Francis, "Christmas Address to the Roman Curia," December 21, 2020, http://www.vatican.va. See also Peter De Mey, "Church Renewal and Reform in the Documents of Vatican II: History, Theology, Terminology," *Jurist* 71 (2011): 369–400; Sandra Arenas, "Ecclesial Extroversion: On the Reform in the Current Pontificate," in *Changing the Church: Transformations of Christian Belief, Practice, and Life*, ed. Mark D. Chapman and Vladimir Latinovic (New York: Palgrave MacMillan, 2020), 315–22; Myriam Wijlens, "Reform and Renewal Implementing Vatican II," in *For a Missionary reform of the Church: The Civiltà Cattolica Seminar*, ed. Carlos M. Galli and Antonio Spadaro, SJ (Mahwah, NJ: Paulist Press, 2017), 336–57.

2. Pope Francis, Morning Meditation, "L'acqua che scorre nella chiesa," November 9, 2013, https://www.vatican.va/content/francesco/it/cotidie/2013/documents/papa-francesco-cotidie_20131109_acqua-della-grazia.html.

3. Pope Francis, "Christmas Address to the Roman Curia," December 22, 2014, https://www.vatican.va/content/francesco/en/speeches/2014/december/documents/papa-francesco_20141222_curia-romana.html.

4. Pope Francis, "Christmas Address to the Roman Curia," December 21, 2013, https://www.vatican.va/content/francesco/en/speeches/2013/december/documents/papa-francesco_20131221_auguri-curia-romana.html.

5. Here, Pope Francis refers to the *motu proprio Humanam progressionem*, August 17, 2016, to state that "the organizations that collaborate with him must constantly adapt so that they can better respond to the needs of the men and women whom they are called to serve."

6. "The old story of the Samaritan has been the model of the spirituality of the council. A feeling of boundless sympathy has permeated the whole of it. The attention of our council has been absorbed by the discovery of human needs (and these needs grow in proportion to the greatness which the son of the earth claims for himself)....If

we remember how in everyone we can and must recognize the countenance of Christ (cf. Matt. 25:40), the Son of Man, especially when tears and sorrows make it plain to see, and if we can and must recognize in Christ's countenance the countenance of our heavenly Father—'He who sees me,' Our Lord said, 'sees also the Father' (John 14:9)—our humanism becomes Christianity, our Christianity becomes centered on God; in such sort that we may say, to put it differently: a knowledge of man is a prerequisite for a knowledge of God." Pope Paul VI, "Address of Pope Paul VI during the Last General Meeting of the Second Vatican Council," December 7, 1965, https://www.vatican.va/content/paul-vi/en/speeches/1965/documents/hf_p-vi_spe_19651207_epilogo-concilio.html.

7. The word *pueblo* is used with several meanings, such as *pueblo-pobre* (the poor), *pueblo-nación* (the nation), *pueblo-herido* (institutions and society), *pueblo-fiel* (the faithful). Cf. Rafael Luciani, *Pope Francis and the Theology of the People* (Maryknoll: NY: Orbis Books, 2017).

8. Pope Francis, "Christmas Greetings to the Roman Curia," December 22, 2016, https://www.vatican.va/content/francesco/en/speeches/2016/december/documents/papa-francesco_20161222_curia-romana.html.

9. See Cristián Roncagliolo, "Iglesia en salida: una aproximación teológico pastoral al concepto de Iglesia en *Evangelii Gaudium*," *Teología y Vida* 55 no. 2 (2014): 362. Note John Paul II, postsynodal apostolic exhortation *Ecclesia in Oceania*, November 22, 2001, 19: *AAS* 94 (2002), 390.

10. Interview with Cardinal Léon-Joseph Suenens, "La unidad de la Iglesia en la lógica del Vaticano II: El cardenal Suenens contesta las preguntas de José Broucker," *El Ciervo* 18, no. 184 (1969): 4, https://www.jstor.org/stable/40803679.

11. See CELAM, *Renovación y reestructuración del CELAM: Documento de Trabajo* (Bogotá: Celam Press, 2021).

12. Pope Francis, "Address during the Apostolic Journey to Rio de Janeiro to the Leadership of the Episcopal Conferences of Latin America during the General Coordination Meeting," July 28, 2013,

https://www.vatican.va/content/francesco/en/speeches/2013/july/documents/papa-francesco_20130728_gmg-celam-rio.html.

13. Rahner described the relevance of the Council in the following terms: "This is the way things are: either the Church will see and recognize the essential differences of other cultures, within which it must become a global Church, and draw from this recognition the necessary consequences with Pauline audacity, or else it will remain permanently a Western Church and thus betray the meaning of Vatican II." Karl Rahner, "Theologische Grundinterpretation des II. Vatikanischen Konzils," in *Schriften zur Theologie. Band 14* (Einsiedeln: Benzinger Verlag, 1980), 298.

14. The best study on the implications of Canon 129, §2 regarding this topic is Myriam Wijlens, "Ecclesial Lay Ministry, Clergy and Complementarity," *CLSA Proceedings* 64 (2002) 27–47. Esp. see 30–34. As she explains, the exercise of power of jurisdiction without power of order has been understood as dispensing power of the laity, or as the capacity of a layperson to hold a position. But she states that canon lawyers and theologians have been asking the wrong question. The word *cooperation* does not mean to participate, and laity cannot be understood as the nonordained, because the reasoning still centers on the ordination. Therefore, the correct question is whether baptism and confirmation are necessary and sufficient to exercise power of governance.

CHAPTER 3

1. See Pope Francis, "Speech at the Commemoration of the 50th Anniversary of the Institution of the Synod of Bishops," October 17, 2015, https://www.vatican.va/content/francesco/en/speeches/2015/october/documents/papa-francesco_20151017_50-anniversario-sinodo.html.

2. See Pope Paul VI, "Speech at the Beginning of Labors in the Synodal Hall," *Synodus Episcoporum*, September 30, 1967, https://www.vatican.va/content/paul-vi/it/speeches/1967/september/documents/hf_p-vi_spe_19670930_inizio-lavori-sinodo.html.

Notes

3. International Theological Commission, "Synodality in the Life and Mission of the Church," March 2, 2018, no. 6, https://www.vatican.va/roman_curia/congregations/cfaith/cti_documents/rc_cti_20180302_sinodalita_en.html.

4. See Rafael Luciani, "Lo que afecta a todos debe ser tratado y aprobado por todos. Hacia estructuras de participación y poder de decisión compartido," *Revista CLAR* LVIII, no. 1 (2020): 59–66.

5. See Winfried Aymans, "Sinodalità: forma di governo ordinaria o straordinaria nella Chiesa," in Winfried Aymans, *Diritto canonico e comunione ecclesiale. Saggi di diritto canonico in prospecttiva theologica* (Torino: Giappichelli Editore, 1993), 40.

6. See Carlos M. Galli, "La figura sinodal de la Iglesia según la Comisión Teológica Internacional," in *En camino hacia una Iglesia Sinodal: de Pablo VI a Francisco*, ed. María Teresa Compte and Rafael Luciani (Madrid: PPC, 2020), 120–22.

7. Gaudenzio Zamnon, "Riconoscimento reciproco di soggettività tra laici e ministri ordinati in ordine ad una forma sinodale di chiesa," in *Chiesa e sinodalità*, ed. Ricardo Battocchio and Serena Noceti (Milano: Glossa, 2007), 194.

8. Bernard Franck, "Les expériences synodales après Vatican II," *Communio* 3, no. 3 (1978): 77.

9. Franck, "Les expériences synodales après Vatican II," 77.

10. Pope Francis, "Speech in Commemoration of the 50th Anniversary of the Institution of the Synod of Bishops."

11. Alphonse Borras, "Trois expressions de la synodalité depuis Vatican II," *Ephemerides Theologicae Lovanienses* 90, no. 4 (2014): 648.

12. Pope Francis, "Christmas Greetings to the Roman Curia," December 22, 2016, https://www.vatican.va/content/francesco/en/speeches/2016/december/documents/papa-francesco_20161222_curia-romana.html.

13. The pope indicated twelve principles that should guide such a process of reform and conversion: "individuality (personal conversion); pastoral sense (pastoral conversion); missionary commitment (Christ-centeredness); rationality; functionality; modernity (staying

up-to-date); sobriety; subsidiarity; synodality; catholicity; professionalism; and gradualism (discernment)."

14. Borras, "Trois expressions de la synodalité depuis Vatican II,"
650.

15. "In the synodal Church *the whole community*, in the free
and rich diversity of its members, is called together to pray, listen,
analyse, dialogue, discern and offer advice *on taking pastoral decisions*
which correspond as closely as possible to God's will." International
Theological Commission, "Synodality in the Life and Mission of the
Church," no. 68.

16. Antonio Lanfranchi notes, "It does not depend simply and
first of all on the good functioning of the various organisms or on
simple criteria of democratic participation, such as the criterion of
the majority, but requires from its members an ecclesial awareness, a
style of fraternal communication, which translates communion and the
common convergence on a project of the Church," "Prassi spirituale del
discernimento comunitaria," in Battocchio and Noceti, *Chiesa e sinodalità*, 194.

CHAPTER 4

1. International Theological Commission, "Synodality in the
Life and Mission of the Church," March 2, 2018. no. 68, https://www
.vatican.va/roman_curia/congregations/cfaith/cti_documents/rc_cti
_20180302_sinodalita_en.html.

2. International Theological Commission, "Synodality in the
Life and Mission of the Church," no. 67.

3. Gaudenzio Zamnon, "Riconoscimento reciproco di soggettività tra laici e ministri ordinati in ordine ad una forma sinodale di
chiesa," in *Chiesa e sinodalità*, ed. Ricardo Battocchio and Serena Noceti
(Milano: Glossa, 2007), 194.

4. "Synodality is lived out in the Church in the service of mission. *Ecclesia peregrinans natura sua missionaria est*; she exists in order
to evangelise. The whole People of God is an agent of the proclamation

of the Gospel. Every baptized person is called to be a protagonist of mission since we are all missionary disciples. The Church is called, in synodal synergy, to activate the ministries and charisms present in her life and to listen to the voice of the Spirit, in order to discern the ways of evangelization." International Theological Commission, "Synodality in the Life and Mission of the Church," no. 53.

5. International Theological Commission, "Synodality in the Life and Mission of the Church," no. 106.

6. "Three actions or practices specifically describe what dialogue is: *expressing opinions, listening, and taking counsel.*" See Gilles Routhier, "La synodalitè dans l'Église locale," *Scripta Theologica* 48, no. 3 (2016): 695–96.

7. Routhier, "La synodalitè dans l'Église locale," 700–701.

8. International Theological Commission, "Synodality in the Life and Mission of the Church," no. 69.

9. International Theological Commission, "Synodality in the Life and Mission of the Church," no. 72.

10. International Theological Commission, "Synodality in the Life and Mission of the Church," no. 94.

11. Cf. Juan Ignacio Arrieta, "Órganos de participación y corresponsabilidad en la Iglesia diocesana," *Ius Canonicum* 34, no. 68 (1994): 553–93.

12. Cf. Francesco Coccopalmerio, "La natura della consultività ecclesiale," in *Partecipazione e corresponsabilità nella Chiesa,* ed. Mauro Rivella (Milano: Ancora, 2000), 23–31.

13. "La unidad de la Iglesia en la lógica del Vaticano II: El cardenal Suenens contesta las preguntas de José Broucker." Interview with Cardinal Léon-Joseph Suenens, "La unidad de la Iglesia en la lógica del Vaticano II: El cardenal Suenens contesta las preguntas de José Broucker," *El Ciervo* 18, no. 184 (1969): 7, https://www.jstor.org/stable/40803679.

14. Severino Dianich, *Riforma della Chiesa e ordinamento canonico* (Bologna: EDB, 2018), 69–70.

CHAPTER 5

1. "An image of the Church that pleases me is that of a holy people, faithful to God. It is the definition I often use, and it is also the definition of *Lumen Gentium* in paragraph 12." Interview with Pope Francis by Antonio Spadaro, SJ, 2013, https://www.vatican.va/archive/hist _councils/ii_vatican_council/documents/vat-ii_const_19641121 _lumen-gentium_en.html.

2. León Joseph Suenens, *Coresponsibility in the Church* (New York: Herder and Herder, 1968), 30.

3. See Serena Noceti, "Elaborare decisioni nella chiesa. Una riflessione ecclesiologica," in *Sinodalità. Dimensione della Chiesa, pratiche nella chiesa*, ed. Riccardo Battocchio and Livio Tonello (Padova: EMP, 2020), 237–54.

4. Yves Congar, "The Church: The People of God," *Concilium* 1, no. 1 (1965): 12–13. A general outline of the debates on the notion of people of God during the Council and in the immediate postcouncil period can be found in the first chapter of Hermanus Wilhelmus María Rikhof, *The Concept of Church: A Methodological Inquiry into the Use of Metaphors in Ecclesiology* (London: Sheed & Ward Ltd. and Patmos Press, 1981).

5. Cf. *Acta Synodalia Sacrosancti Concilii Oecumenici Vaticani II*, 32 vols. (Vatican City: Typis Polyglottis Vaticanis, 1970–99), 1/4, 143.

6. International Theological Commission, "Synodality in the Life and Mission of the Church," March 2, 2018, no.54, https://www .vatican.va/roman_curia/congregations/cfaith/cti_documents/rc_cti _20180302_sinodalita_en.html.

7. Cf. Alberto Parra, "El proceso de sacerdotalización. Una histórica interpretación de los ministerios eclesiales," *Theologica Xaveriana* 28, no. 1 (1978): 79–100.

8. Pope Francis, "Christmas Greeting to the Roman Curia," December 21, 2013, https://www.vatican.va/content/francesco/en/ speeches/2013/december/documents/papa-francesco_20131221 _auguri-curia-romana.html.

Notes

9. Pope Francis, "Letter to the Whole People of God in Chile, May 2018," in Jorge Mario Bergoglio, *Letters of Tribulation*, ed. Antonio Spadaro, SJ, and Diego Fares (Maryknoll, NY: Orbis Books, 2019).

10. Pope Francis, "Letter to the Whole People of God in Chile, May 2018."

11. Cf. *Acta Synodalia Sacrosancti Concilii Oecumenici Vaticani II*, 1/4, 142–44.

12. Cf. *Acta Synodalia Sacrosancti Concilii Oecumenici Vaticani II*, 1/4, 143.

13. Gilles Routhier, "Évangilie et modèle de sociabilité," *Laval Théologique et Philosophique* 51, no. 1 (1995): 69.

14. Cf. Serena Noceti, "La costituzione gerarchica della Chiesa e in particolare l'episcopato," in *Commentario ai documenti del Vaticano II*, vol. 2, ed. Serena Noceti and Roberto Repole (Bologna: EDB, 2015), 216.

15. Suenens, *Coresponsibility in the Church*, 10.

16. Interview with Cardinal Léon-Joseph Suenens: "La unidad de la Iglesia en la lógica del Vaticano II. El cardenal Suenens contesta las preguntas de José Broucker," 5.

17. Cf. *Lumen Gentium* 13: "In virtue of this catholicity each individual part contributes through its special gifts to the good of the other parts and of the whole Church. Through the common sharing of gifts and through the common effort to attain fullness in unity, the whole and each of the parts receive increase. Not only, then, is the people of God made up of different peoples, but it is also composed of various ranks in its inner structure. This diversity among its members arises either by reason of their duties, as is the case with those who exercise the sacred ministry for the good of their brethren, or by reason of their condition and state of life, as is the case with those many who enter the religious state and, tending toward holiness by a narrower path, stimulate their brethren by their example."

18. Pope Francis, "Speech in Commemoration of the 50th Anniversary of the Institution of the Synod of Bishops."

19. "Synodality not only proposes a model of exchange and coordination but above all allows everyone to participate in the common

work, according to their rank. Therefore, this concept, while taking into account the diversity of functions, guarantees an orderly and organic participation that is not guaranteed by coresponsibility. Synodality has the merit of correctly encouraging the participation of all according to the diversity and originality of gifts and services. More specifically, synodality expresses the state of each person as that state flows from the sacraments: baptism-confirmation and orders." Translated from Gilles Routhier, "Évangilie et modèle de sociabilité," *Laval Théologique et Philosophique* 51, no. 1 (1995): 69.

20. Pope Francis, "Speech at the Commemoration of the 50th Anniversary of the Institution of the Synod of Bishops."

21. Juan Fornés, "Notas sobre el 'Duo sunt genera Christianorum' del *Decreto de Graciano*," *Ius Canonicum* 30, no. 60 (1990): 607–32. See especially 622–23, concerning the shift from the medieval Christendom system—which established a twofold hierarchical structure, ecclesiastical and secular, based on power—to recognizing the radical equality of all as Christians, *Christifideles*, exercising different functions.

22. Emile-Joseph De Smedt, *The Priesthood of the Faithful* (New York: Paulist Press, 1962), 115.

23. To understand the different hermeneutics being applied to the Council before Francis became pope, see Carlos Schickendantz, "Estudios sistemático-hermenéuticos sobre el Vaticano II: Tres aportes relevantes en el período posconciliar," *Veritas* 30 (2014): 187–211.

24. "The Church is not one Pontiff, nor is it the Pontiff with the hierarchical order. *The Church is all the faithful* baptized in Christ. All persons, even those not baptized, are *potentially* members of Christ." *AD I / II, VII,* 25.

CHAPTER 6

1. *Schemata Constitutionum et Decretorum de quibus disceptabitur in Concilii sessionibus: De Ecclesia et de B. Maria Virgine,* part 2 (Vatican City: Typis Polyglottis Vaticanis, 1962), 37.

Notes

2. "Although the ministerial or juridical priesthood is different from the universal priesthood of the faithful in essence and not only in degree, still, they both proceed, each in its own way, from the high priesthood of Christ, and they are mutually ordained one to the other." *Schemata Constitutionum et Decretorum de quibus disceptabitur in Concilii sessionibus. Schema Constitutionis Dogmaticae Ecclesiae*, part 2 (Vatican City: Typis Polyglottis Vaticanis, 1963), 7.

3. *Schema Constitutionis De Ecclesia*, 43.

4. "Pro parte consideratur ut proprium, sed analogicum. Quaestio tamen non videtur hic dirimenda. Diffierentia inter utrumque sacerdotium suo loco exponitur." See *Schema Constitutionis De Ecclesia*, 42.

5. Cf. *Acta Synodalia Sacrosancti Concilii Oecumenici Vaticani II*, 32 vols. (Vatican City: Typis Polyglottis Vaticanis, 1970–99), II/1, 324–29.

6. Cf. Salvador Pié-Ninot, *La sacramentalidad de la comunidad cristiana* (Salamanca: Cristiandad, 2007), 289–331.

7. Cf. *Acta Synodalia Sacrosancti Concilii Oecumenici Vaticani II*, 1/4, 143.

8. Santiago Madrigal, *Unas lecciones sobre el Vaticano II y su legado* (Madrid: San Pablo, 2012), 278.

9. "From the point of view of ecclesial practice, the lack of reception of the relationship of circularity between the common priesthood and the ministerial priesthood as two complementary forms of participation in the priesthood of Christ, clearly drawn by LG 10; from the point of view of ecclesiological reflection, the risk of distorting the conciliar doctrine due to the inability to attribute the common priesthood not to the individual baptized (with relative emphasis on the slogan that 'we are all priests'), but to the 'priestly community,' to the '*universitas fidelium*' as the subject of ecclesial action which finds its happiest expression in the exercise of the *sensus omnium fidelium* proposed in LG 12." Translated from Dario Vitali, "Il Popolo di Dio," in *Commentario ai documenti del Vaticano II*, vol. 2, ed. Serena Noceti and Roberto Repole (Bologna: EDB, Bologna, 2015), 167.

10. It is worth recalling that the Note was signed by the secretary general of the Council and not by the president of the commission. It was read to the conciliar fathers on November 16, one day before the final vote on the third chapter of *Lumen Gentium*. Regarding the Note, there could be no discussion or vote.

11. Pope Paul VI, "Apostolic Letter Issued Motu proprio *Apostolica Sollicitudo*" (September 15, 1965), establishing the Synod of Bishops for the Universal Church, https://www.vatican.va/content/paul-vi/en/motu_proprio/documents/hf_p-vi_motu-proprio_19650915_apostolica-sollicitudo.html.

12. Pope Paul VI, "Apostolic Letter Issued Motu proprio *Sollicitudo Omnium Ecclesiarum*" (June 24, 1969), regarding the Office of the Representatives of the Roman Pontiff, https://www.vatican.va/content/paul-vi/it/motu_proprio/documents/hf_p-vi_motu-proprio_19690624_sollicitudo-omnium-ecclesiarum.html.

13. Pope Francis, "Address at the Commemoration of the 50th Anniversary of the Institution of the Synod of Bishops," October 17, 2015.

14. Bernardo Bayona Aznar, "Nacimiento, letargo y renacimiento de la colegialidad en el Concilio Vaticano II," *Didaskalia* 45 no. 1 (2015): 117–34.

15. Cf. Carlos María Galli, "La figura sinodal de la Iglesia según la Comisión Teológica Internacional," in *La sinodalidad en la vida de la Iglesia: Reflexiones para contribuir a la reforma eclesial*, 17–40.

16. Pedro Trigo, *Concilio Plenario Venezolano: Una constituyente para nuestras Iglesia* (Caracas: Centro Gumilla, 2009), 329.

17. Pope Francis, "Letter to the People of God," August 20, 2018, https://www.vatican.va/content/francesco/en/letters/2018/documents/papa-francesco_20180820_lettera-popolo-didio.html.

18. Cardinal León Joseph Suenens, *Coresponsibility in the Church* (New York: Herder and Herder, 1968), 211.

19. Carlos Schickendantz, "La reforma de la Iglesia en clave sinodal. Una agenda compleja y articulada," *Teología y Vida* 58, no. 1 (2017): 43.

Notes

20. See Serena Noceti, "*Sensus Fidelium* and the Ecclesial Dynamics," in *Authentic Voices, Discerning Hearts*, ed. Thomas Knieps-Port le Roi and A. Brenninkmeijer-Werhahn (Zürich: LIT Verlag, 2016), 170–83.

CHAPTER 7

1. See Hervé Legrand, "Lo sviluppo di chiese-soggetto: un'istanza del Vaticano II," *Cristianesimo nella Storia* 2, no. 1 (1981): 152–53.

2. International Theological Commission, "Synodality in the Life and Mission of the Church," March 2, 2018, no. 90, https://www.vatican.va/roman_curia/congregations/cfaith/cti_documents/rc_cti_20180302_sinodalita_en.html.

3. International Theological Commission, "Synodality in the Life and Mission of the Church," no. 69.

4. International Theological Commission, "Synodality in the Life and Mission of the Church," no. 64.

5. International Theological Commission, "Synodality in the Life and Mission of the Church," no. 64.

6. Cardinal León Joseph Suenens, *Coresponsibility in the Church* (New York: Herder and Herder, 1968), 191.

7. Eugenio Corecco, "Struttura sinodale o democratica della Chiesa particolare," in *Ius et Communio. Scritti di Diritto Canonico*, II, ed. Graziano Borgonovo and Arturo Cattaneo (Casale Monferrato: Piemme, 1997), 18.

8. Daniel J. Finucane, *Sensus Fidelium: The Use of a Concept in the Post–Vatican II Era* (Eugene, OR: Wipf & Stock, 1996/2016).

9. International Theological Commission, "Synodality in the Life and Mission of the Church," no. 64.

10. This can also be appreciated in the Synod for the Youth, as exposed by Nathalie Becquart, "The Synod on Young People, a Laboratory of Synodality," *International Bulletin of Mission Research* (2020): 1–16.

11. International Theological Commission, "Synodality in the Life and Mission of the Church," no. 60.

12. International Theological Commission, "Synodality in the Life and Mission of the Church," no. 107.

13. See Rafael Luciani, "Lo que afecta a todos debe ser tratado y aprobado por todos: Hacia estructuras de participación y poder de decisión compartido," *Revista CLAR* 58, no. 1 (2020): 59–66.

14. *Schemata Constitutionum et Decretorum de quibus disceptabitur in Concilii Sessionibus. Schema Decreti De Apostolatu Laicorum* (Vatican City: Typis Polyglottis Vaticanis, 1963), 5.

15. *Schema Decreti De Apostolatu Laicorum*, 1964, 6.

16. *Schema Decreti De Apostolatu Laicorum. Textus recognitus et modi a Patribus Conciliaribus propositi a Commissione de fidelium apostolatu examinati* (Vatican City: Typis Polyglottis Vaticanis, 1965), 23.

17. See Gaudenzio Zamnon, "Riconoscimento reciproco di soggettività tra laici e ministri ordinati in ordine ad una forma sinodale di chiesa," in *Chiesa e sinodalità*, ed. Ricardo Battocchio and Serena Noceti (Milano: Glossa, 2007), 194.

18. See José R. Villar, "Identidad secular del laico en el mundo," in *Laicado y misión* (Madrid: PPC, 2017), 66–69.

19. See Antonio José de Almeida, "Laicos y laicas en la práctica de la sinodalidad," in *Reforma de estructuras y conversión de mentalidades. Retos y desafíos para una Iglesia Sinodal*, ed. Rafael Luciani (Madrid: KHAF, 2020), 243–76.

20. "It does not depend simply and first of all on the good functioning of the various organisms or on simple criteria of democratic participation, such as the criterion of the majority, but requires from its members an ecclesial awareness, a style of fraternal communication, which translates communion and the common convergence on a project of the Church." Translated from Antonio Lanfranchi, "Prassi spirituale del discernimento comunitario," in *Chiesa e sinodalità*, ed. Riccardo Battocchio and Serena Noceti (Milan: Glossa, 2007), 194.

21. Suenens, *Coresponsibility in the Church*, 176.

22. Severino Dianich, "Dalla teologia della sinodalità alla riforma della normativa canonica," in *La sinodalità nella vita e nella missione della Chiesa: Commento a più voci al Documento della Commissione teologica*

internazionale, ed. Piero Coda and Roberto Repole (Bologna: EDB, 2019), 75.

23. See Yves Congar, "Quod omnes tangit ab omnibus tractari et opprobari debet," *Revue historique de droit français et étranger* 36 (1958): 210–59.

24. Alphonse Borras, "Sinodalità ecclesiale, processi partecipati e modalità decisionali," in *La riforma e le riforme nella Chiesa,* ed. Carlos María Galli and Antonio Spadaro (Brescia: Queriniana, 2016), 232.

CHAPTER 8

1. International Theological Commission, "Synodality in the Life and Mission of the Church," March 2, 2018, no. 42, https://www .vatican.va/roman_curia/congregations/cfaith/cti_documents/rc_cti _20180302_sinodalita_en.html.

2. Emile-Joseph De Smedt, *The Priesthood of the Faithful* (New York: Paulist Press, 1962), 89–90.

3. Pope Francis, "Address at the Commemoration of the 50th Anniversary of the Institution of the Synod of Bishops," October 17, 2015.

4. Santiago Madrigal, *Unas lecciones sobre el Vaticano II y su legado* (Madrid: San Pablo, 2012), 234.

5. See Rafael Luciani, "Reforma, conversión pastoral y sinodalidad. Un nuevo modo eclesial de proceder," in *La sinodalidad en la vida de la Iglesia,* ed. Rafael Luciani and María del Pilar Silveira (Madrid: San Pablo, 2020), 41–66.

6. Dario Vitali, *Lumen Gentium: Storia, Commento, Recezione* (Rome: Studium, 2012), 67.

7. Cf. Vitali, *Lumen Gentium: Storia, Commento, Recezione,* 67; Myriam Wijlens, "Primacy-Collegiality-Synodality: Reconfiguring the Church because of *sensus fidei,*" in *Proceedings of the 23rd Congress of the Eastern Churches,* ed. Peter Szabo, Debrecen, September 3–8, 2017, *Kanan XXV* (2019), 237–60; Dario Vitali, "The Circularity between *Sensus Fidei* and Magisterium as a Criterion for the Exercise of Synodality in the Church," in *For a Missionary Reform of the Church: The*

Civiltà Cattolica Seminar, ed. Carlos M. Galli and Antonio Spadaro, SJ (Mahwah, NJ: Paulist Press, 2017), 196–217; and Herve Legrand, "Reception, *Sensus fidelium,* and Synodal Life: An Effort at Articulation," *Jurist* 57, no. 1 (1997): 405–31.

8. Peter Hünermann, "Lumen Gentium kommentiert von Peter Hünerman," in *Herders Theologischer Kommentar zum Zweiten Vatikanischen Konzil,* vol. 2, ed. Peter Hünermann und Bernd Jochen Hilberath (Freiburg: Herder, 2004), 440.

9. Karl Rahner, *The Shape of the Church to Come* (London: SPCK, 1974), 38.

10. See "Verso una chiesa mondiale," in *Modelli di chiesa,* ed. G. Canobbio, F. Dalla Vecchia, and R. Tononi (Brescia: Morcelliana, 2001), 67–94.

11. Antonio Lanfranchi, "Prassi spirituale del discernimento comunitario," in *Chiesa e sinodalità,* ed. Riccardo Battocchio and Serena Noceti (Milan: Glossa, 2007), 194.

12. Alphonse Borras, "*Votum tantum consultivum.* Les limites ecclesiologiques d'une formule canonique," *Didaskalia* 45, no. 1 (2015): 161.

13. International Theological Commission, "Synodality in the Life and Mission of the Church," no. 68.

14. "When I decided from the beginning of my episcopate, *in private and without your consent, so shall ye be my own opinion, without the consent of the people, there is nothing to carry on,*" translated from the Latin in *Patrologia Latina,* vol. 4, Jacques Paul Migne (S. Cypriani), 234.

15. International Theological Commission, "Synodality in the Life and Mission of the Church," no. 69.

16. Alphonse Borras, "Sinodalità ecclesiale, processi partecipati e modalità decisionali," in *La riforma e le riforme nella Chiesa,* ed. Carlos María Galli and Antonio Spadaro, SJ (Brescia: Queriniana, 2016), 231–32.

17. International Theological Commission, "Synodality in the Life and Mission of the Church," no. 76.

Notes

18. International Theological Commission, "Synodality in the Life and Mission of the Church," no. 106.

19. Borras, "Votum tantum consultivum," 161.

20. "The teaching body [bishops] did not receive from the beginning a perfectly explicit expression of Catholic truths that it gradually presented to the People of God. In the Church there is a certain development of doctrine. Is this more profound vision of the Gospel achieved only by the action of the Holy Spirit on the bishops? No, *the whole Church*—bishops and faithful—are in a certain sense *involved in this growth in understanding* of the Word." De Smedt, *The Priesthood of the Faithful*, 89–90.

21. Karl Rahner, *Strukturwandel der Kirche als Aufgabe und Chance* (Freiburg-Basel-Wien: Herder, 1972), 78–79.

22. See Yves Marie Congar, "Quod omnes tangit ab omnibus tractari et opprobari debet," *Revue historique de droit français et étranger* 36, no. 4 (1958): 210–59.

23. See Luciani, "Lo que afecta a todos debe ser tratado y aprobado por todos," 59–66.

24. Ronaldo Muñoz, *Nueva conciencia de la Iglesia en América Latina* (Salamanca: Sígueme, 1974), 363.

25. International Theological Commission, "Synodality in the Life and Mission of the Church."

26. Serena Noceti, "Elaborare decisioni nella chiesa. Una riflessione ecclesiologica," in *Sinodalità. Dimensione della Chiesa, pratiche nella chiesa*, ed. Riccardo Battocchio and Livio Tonello (Padova: EMP, 2020), 253.

27. Madrigal, *Unas lecciones sobre el Vaticano II y su legado*, 234.

28. Pope Francis, "Speech at the Meeting with Priests, Religious, and Seminarians in the Coliseum of the Colegio Don Bosco," Santa Cruz de la Sierra, Bolivia, July 9, 2015, https://www.vatican .va/content/francesco/en/speeches/2015/july/documents/papa -francesco_20150709_bolivia-religiosi.html.

29. According to Bishop Fernández, "The subject of the *sensus fidelium* could be simply the sum of individuals who believe the same truths.

In contrast, the *sensus populi* has a collective subject, the People, who on the basis of their shared Christian experience express themselves by producing a singular culture that provides others with access to that same experience: the People evangelize the People." See Víctor Manuel Fernández, "El sensus populi: la legitimidad de una teología desde el pueblo," *Teología* 72 (1998): 162.

30. Juan Landázuri Ricketts, "Inaugural Speech (of Medellín)," in *La Iglesia en la actual transformación de América Latina a la luz del Concilio. Ponencias*, Consejo Episcopal Latinoamericano, Bogotá, 1968, 47.

31. "Interview with Pope Francis," by Antonio Spadaro, SJ, 2013, https://www.vatican.va/content/francesco/en/speeches/2013/september/documents/papa-francesco_20130921_intervista-spadaro.html.

CHAPTER 9

1. International Theological Commission, "Synodality in the Life and Mission of the Church," March 2, 2018, no. 77, https://www.vatican.va/roman_curia/congregations/cfaith/cti_documents/rc_cti_20180302_sinodalita_en.html.

2. Avery Dulles, "Catholic Ecclesiology since Vatican II," in *Synod 1985: An Evaluation*, ed. Giuseppe Alberigo and James Provost (Edinburgh: Concilium and T&T Clark, 1986), 12.

3. See Avery Dulles, *Church and Society: The Laurence J. McGinley Lectures, 1988–2007* (New York: Fordham University Press, 2008), 475–78.

4. See Congregation for the Doctrine of the Faith, "*Communionis notio*: Letter to the Bishops of the Catholic Church on Certain Aspects of the Church Understood as Communion," May 28, 1992, no. 9.

5. Walter Kasper, "Das Verhältnis von Universalkirche und Ortskirche. Freundschaftliche Auseinandersetzung mit der Kritik von Joseph Kardinal Ratzinger," *Stimmen der Zeit* 218 (2000): 795–804; Joseph Ratzinger, "L'ecclesiologia della Costituzione Lumen Gentium,"

Notes

in *Concilio Vaticano II: Recezione e attualità alla luce del Giubileo*, ed.
Rino Fisichella (Cinisello Balsamo: San Paolo, 2000), 66–81.

6. Salvador Pié-Ninot, "Ecclesia in et ex Ecclesiis (LG 23): La
catolicidad de la Communio Ecclesiarum," *RCat* 22, no. 1 (1997): 87.

7. Karl Rahner and Joseph Ratzinger, *Episcopado y primado*
(Barcelona: Herder, 1961/2005), 28.

8. We can therefore state that "the diocese is a portion of the
People of God, fully endowed on the theological plane with all its
goods....In and from [the diocesan churches] comes into being the
one and only Catholic Church (LG 23). For this reason, together with
many other theologians, I believe it is necessary to preserve in theology
the traditional expression of the diocesan or even the local Church." See
Hervé Legrand, "L'articolazione tra le Chiese locali, Chiese regionali e
Chiesa universale," *Ad gentes: teologia e antropologia della missione* 3, no.
1 (1999): 19.

9. "Presentation of the Programme for the celebration of the
upcoming Synod approved by Pope Francis during his audience with
Cardinal Secretary General of the Synod of Bishops," April 24, 2021,
http://secretariat.synod.va/content/synod/en/news/document-of
-the-synodal-process--xvi-ordinary-general-assembly-o.html.

10. "The universal Church that is realized in the local churches is
the same Church that is constituted on the basis of the local churches.
Thus, the formula *in quibus et ex quibus* captures the mystery of the
Church and its institutional essence, in accord with the logic of the
reciprocal immanence of the local-particular dimension in the universal-
Catholic dimension and vice versa." Salvador Pié-Ninot, "Ecclesia in et
ex Ecclesiis (LG 23): La catolicidad de la Communio Ecclesiarum," 78.

11. See Gérard Philips, *La Iglesia y su misterio en el Concilio Vaticano II. Historia y comentario de la Constitución Lumen Gentium*, vol. 1
(Barcelona: Herder, 1968), 383.

12. J.-J. von Allmen, "L'Église locale parmi les autres Églises
locales," *Irénikon* 43, no. 4 (1970): 512.

13. Hervé Legrand, "Iglesia(s) local(es), Iglesias regionales o particulares, Iglesia católica," in *Iglesia universal. Iglesias particulares*, ed. J. C. Scannone et al. (Buenos Aires: San Pablo, 2000), 133.

14. "Either the Church will see and recognize the essential differences of these other cultures within which it must become a world Church and will, with Pauline boldness, draw the necessary consequences from that recognition, or it will remain in the end a Western Church, thus betraying the meaning of Vatican II." Karl Rahner, "Theologische Grundinterpretation des II. Vatikanischen Konzils," in *Schriften zur Theologie*, vol. 14 (Einsiedeln: Benzinger Verlag, 1980), 298. See also Yves Congar, "Propiedades esenciales de la Iglesia," in *Mysterium Salutis: Manual de teología como historia de la salvación*, ed. M. Löhrer and J. Feiner, vol. 4/1, 2nd. ed. (Madrid; Cristiandad 1984), 510–13.

15. Agenor Brighenti, "Sinodalidad eclesial y colegialidad episcopal. El referente del estatuto teológico de las conferencias episcopales," in *La sinodalidad en la vida de la Iglesia*, ed. Rafael Luciani and María del Pilar Silveira (Madrid: San Pablo, 2020), 100.

16. See Rafael Luciani, "El proceso de autocomprensión misionera de la Iglesia en América Latina: Desarrollo de una eclesiología ambiental en clave misionera," *Revista Fronteiras* 4, no. 1 (2021): 62–104.

17. Legrand, "Iglesia(s) local(es), Iglesias regionales o particulares, Iglesia católica," 139.

18. See Jean-Marie Tillard, *L'Église locale. Ecclésiologie de communion et catholicité* (Paris: Editions du Cerf, 1995).

19. Legrand, "Iglesia(s) local(es), Iglesias regionales o particulares, Iglesia católica," 138.

20. See Luciani, "El proceso de autocomprensión misionera de la Iglesia en América Latina: Desarrollo de una eclesiología ambiental en clave misionera," 62–104.

21. Lucio Gera, "Puebla: evangelización de la cultura," *Teología* 16, no. 33 (1979): 79.

22. Christoph Theobald, "The Principle of Pastorality," in *The Legacy of Vatican II*, ed. Massimo Faggioli and Andrea Vicini (Mahwah, NJ: Paulist Press 2015), 28.

23. See Christoph Theobald, *Le Concile Vatican II: Quel avenir?* (Paris: Editions du Cerf, 2015). See chap. 3.

24. International Theological Commission, "Synodality in the Life and Mission of the Church," 61.

25. International Theological Commission, "Synodality in the Life and Mission of the Church," 61.

26. International Theological Commission, "Synodality in the Life and Mission of the Church," 52.

CHAPTER 10

1. "The local Churches will be fully Catholic only at the end of a process of inculturation." Hervé Legrand, "La Chiesa si realizza in un luogo," in *Iniziazione alla pratica della teologia*, ed. B. Lauret and F. Refoulé, 2nd ed. (Brescia: Queriniana, 1992), 157.

2. Gilles Routhier, "La synodalitè dans l'Église locale," *Scripta Theologica* 48, no. 3 (2016): 701.

3. See Rafael Luciani, "Medellín Fifty Years Later: From Development to Liberation," in *Theological Studies* 79, no. 3 (2018): 566–89.

4. Alberto M. Ferré, "Del Vaticano II a Medellin (1962–1968)," in *Consejo Episcopal Latino-Americano. CELEM: Elementos para su historia* (Bogotá: Consejo Episcoipal Latinoamericano, 1982); see also http://metholferre.com.

5. Cecilio De Lora, "Del Concilio a Medellín, hoy," in *Horizonte* 9, no. 24 (2011): 1234.

6. Juan Landázuri Ricketts, "Discurso de clausura de la II Conferencia General del Episcopado Latinoamericano," in *Signos de renovación. Recopilación de documentos post-conciliares de la Iglesia en América Latina* (Lima: Comisión Episcopal de Acción Social, 1969), 250–51, 252.

7. Jorge Mejía, "El pequeño Concilio de Medellín (II)" *Criterio* 41 (1968): 687.

8. José Oscar Beozzo, "Medellín: Inspiração e raízes," *Revista Eclesiástica Brasileira* 58, no. 232 (1998): 833.

9. J. Álvarez Calderón, "En ruta hacia Medellín," *Páginas*, 8, no. 58 (1983): 19.

10. "Synodality is a jurisdictional modality by which the unity of the bishops is guaranteed within the *communio ecclesiarum* at the level of authoritative interpretation of the Word"; "the juridically binding force of its collegial judgments and decisions is not the fruit of the formal force of the principle of majority but rather is a phenomenon of the bishops' convergence among themselves." Eugenio Corecco, "Sinodalitá," in *Nuovo Dizionario di Teologia*, ed. Giuseppe Barbaglio and Severino Dianich, 2nd ed. (Roma: Edizioni Paoline, 1979), 1487.

11. Ricketts, "Discurso de clausura de la II Conferencia General del Episcopado Latinoamericano," 248.

12. See Juan Botero Restrepo, *Celam. Elementos para su historia* (Bogotá: Editorial Copiyepes, 1982), 166.

13. José Oscar Beozzo, *A Igreja do Brasil no Concílio Vaticano II: 1959–1965* (São Paulo: Paulinas, 2005), 537.

14. Ricketts, "Discurso de clausura de la II Conferencia General del Episcopado Latinoamericano," 249.

15. Ricketts, "Discurso de clausura de la II Conferencia General del Episcopado Latinoamericano," 248.

16. Mejía, "El pequeño Concilio de Medellín," 653.

17. José Oscar Beozzo, "Medellín: Inspiração e raíces," 833.

18. The text adds that "the first two presentations treated of the 'signs of the times' and how to interpret them as Christians in Latin America. To that end, the assembly adapted the tone and the method of *Gaudium et Spes* as an example to be followed in the whole session." Marcos McGrath, "Algunas reflexiones sobre el impacto y la influencia permanente de Medellín y Puebla en la Iglesia de América Latina," *Medellín* 15, nos. 58–59 (1989): 164.

19. Some 247 people had the right to participate in the assembly, although seven of them could not attend. Of those who attended, 130 were voting members and 110 were participants who had a voice but no vote. The nonvoting group included laypeople, women religious, invited experts, and non-Catholic observers. The topic of voting is

further elucidated in Alberto Múnera, "Crónica de la II Conferencia General del Episcopado Latinoamericano," *Theologica Xaveriana* 349 (1968): 397–98.

20. "The methodology adopted by the assembly for pacing its work was twofold: group meetings and plenary sessions. For the former, the bishops divided themselves according to [which of] the sixteen topics...were of greatest concern to them, and working commissions were set up for each topic. Each commission had the task of working on a document to be submitted to the plenary sessions, where all those attending the assembly would debate what had come forth from the group sessions. Ultimately, then, it was the plenary assembly whose job it was to unify the various topics in order to give them its approval and create the final document." J. Jaramillo Martínez, "Una crónica de Medellín," *Cuestiones Teológicas y Filosóficas* 24, no. 63 (1998): 14–15.

21. C. Tovar, "Quince años de Medellín," *Reflexión* 55 (1983): 16.

22. Samuel Ruiz, "La evangelización en América Latina," in *CELAM: La Iglesia en la actual transformación de América Latina a la luz del Concilio* (Bogotá: Consejo Episcopal Latinoamericano, 1968), 167.

23. Juan Landázuri Ricketts, "Discurso inaugural en Bogotá (August 26, 1968)," in *La Iglesia en la actual transformación de América Latina a la luz del Concilio. Ponencias* (Bogotá: Consejo Episcopal Latinoamericano, 1968).

24. Giorgio Feliciani, *Le conferenze episcopali* (Bologna: Il Mulino, 1974), 291.

25. A "review of the structure" of CELAM was requested in CELAM, *Informe de gestión 2015–2019* (Bogotá: CELAM, 2019), 57.

26. CELAM, *Renovación y reestructuración del CELAM*, April 2021, no. 146, https://issuu.com/conferencia-episcopal-peruana/docs/documento_renovacio_n_y_reestructuracio_n_del_cela.

27. CELAM, *Renovación y reestructuración del CELAM*, no. 163.

28. CELAM, *Renovación y reestructuración del CELAM*, nos. 147–55.

29. CELAM, *Renovación y reestructuración del CELAM*, nos. 184–91.

30. CELAM, *Renovación y reestructuración del CELAM*, no. 147.

31. Cf. Venezuelan Bishops' Conference, *Documentos del Concilio Plenario Venezolano* (Caracas: CEV, 2006); Pedro Trigo, *Concilio Plenario Venezolano: Una constituyente para nuestras Iglesia* (Caracas: Gumilla, 2009); Raúl Biord Castillo, "El Concilio Plenario de Venezuela: Una buena experiencia sinodal," in *En camino hacia una Iglesia sinodal: De Pablo VI a Francisco*, ed. María Teresa Compte and Rafael Luciani (Madrid: PPC, 2020), 77–108.

32. See Alphonse Borras, "La Conférence ecclésiale de l'Amazonie: une institution synodale inédite," *Ephemerides Theologicae Lovanienses* 97, no. 2 (2021): 223–92.

33. See Serena Noceti, *Chiesa, casa comune: Del Sinodo per l'Amazzonia una parola profetica* (Bologna: EDB, 2020), 95–138.

34. Cf. Carlos M. Galli, "Constitución de la Conferencia Eclesial de la Amazonía Fundamentos históricos, teológicos, culturales y pastorales," *Medellín* 46, no. 179 (2020): 517–42.

CONCLUSION

1. Translated from Pope Paul VI, "Discorso all'udienza generale," November 12, 1969, https://w2.vatican.va.

2. Ronaldo Muñoz, *Nueva conciencia de la Iglesia en América Latina* (Salamanca: Sígueme, 1974), 361.

3. See the fundamental analysis in Carlos Schickendantz, "Fracaso institucional de un modelo teológico-cultural de Iglesia. Factores sistémicos en la crisis de los abusos," *Teología y Vida* 60, no. 1 (2019): 9–40.

4. International Theological Commission, "Synodality in the Life and Mission of the Church," March 2, 2018, no. 6, https://www.vatican.va/roman_curia/congregations/cfaith/cti_documents/rc_cti_20180302_sinodalita_en.html.

5. Cardinal Leo Joseph Suenens, *La corresponsabilidad en la Iglesia de hoy* (Bilbao: Desclée de Brouwer, 1969), 27.

6. Muñoz, *Nueva conciencia de la Iglesia en América Latina*, 353.

Notes

7. See John P. Beal, "Consultation in Church Governance: Taking Care of Business by Taking after Business," *Canon Law Society of America. Proceedings* 68 (2006): 25–54.

8. Alphonse Borras, "*Votum tantum consultivum.* Les limites ecclesiologiques d'une formule canonique," *Didaskalia* 45, no. 1 (2015): 161.

9. "Sic collatione consiliorum cum episcopis, presbyteris, diaconis, confessoribus pariter ac stantibus laicis facta, lapsorum tractare rationem…quoniam nec firmum decretum potest esse quod non plurimorum videbitur habuisse consensum," in Jacques Paul Migne, *Patrologiae Latina*, Tomus 4 (S. Cypriani), 312.

10. Severino Dianich, *Diritto e teologia. Ecclesiologia e canonistica per una riforma della Chiesa* (Bologna: EDB, Bologna, 2015), 165.

11. See Rafael Luciani, "Medellín como acontecimiento sinodal: Una eclesialidad colegiada fecundada y completada," *Revista Horizontes* 50 (2018): 482–516.

12. Serena Noceti, "Elaborare decisioni nella chiesa. Una riflessione ecclesiologica," in *Sinodalità. Dimensione della Chiesa, pratiche nella Chiesa*, ed. Riccardo Battocchio and Livio Tonello (Padova: EMP, 2020), 253.

13. Alphonse Borras, "Sinodalità ecclesiale, processi partecipati e modalità decisionali," in *La riforma e le riforme nella Chiesa*, ed. Carlos María Galli and Antonio Spadaro (Brescia: Queriniana, 2016), 231–32.

14. "The problem is compounded when the editorial board doing the filtering is not composed of members of the synod itself, but of conservative advisors appointed by the Vatican." Bradford Hinze, *Practices of Dialogue in the Roman Catholic Church: Aims and Obstacles, Lessons and Laments* (New York: Continuum, 2006), 177.

15. See Yves Congar, "Quod omnes tangit ab omnibus tractari et opprobari debet," *Revue historique de droit français et étranger* 36 (1958): 210–59.

16. Borras, "Sinodalità ecclesiale, processi partecipati e modalità decisionali," 232.

17. For one of the best contributions on the exercise of power in the Church and the participation of the laity in governance, see Laurent Villemin, *Pouvoir d'ordre et pouvoir de juridiction. Histoire théologique de leur distinction* (Paris: Editions du Cerf, 2003).

18. Pope Francis, video message October 8, 2020, https.//www .vaticannews.va/es/papa/news/2020-10/video-papa.html.

19. Yves Congar, *Por una Iglesia servidora y pobre* (Salamanca: San Esteban, 2014), 116–17 (Orig. *Pour une église servant et pauvre* [Paris: Editions du Cerf, Paris 2014]).

20. International Theological Commission, "Synodality in the Life and Mission of the Church," no. 42.

21. Expression used by Eamonn Conway in Royal Commission into Institutional Responses to Child Sexual Abuse, "Religious Institutions," in *Final Report*, vol. 16, bk. 2 (Canberra: Commonwealth of Australia, 2017), 585, https://www.childabuseroyalcommission.gov .au/final-report. See also Schickendantz, "Fracaso institucional de un modelo teológico-cultural de Iglesia," 9–40.

22. See Rafael Luciani, "La reforma como conversión pastoral y sinodal. Eclesiogénesis de una recepción conciliar," in *Reforma de estructuras y conversión de mentalidades. Retos y desafíos para una Iglesia Sinodal*, ed. Rafael Luciani and Carlos Schickendantz (Madrid: KHAF, 2020), 173–202.

23. Muñoz, *Nueva conciencia de la Iglesia en América Latina*, 362.

24. Yves Congar, "Renovación del espíritu y reforma de la institución," *Concilium* 73 (1972): 326–37.

25. Pope Paul VI, "Opening Speech at Vatican II Second Session," September 29, 1963, https://www.vatican.va/content/paul-vi/ it/speeches/1963/documents/hf_p-vi_spe_19630929_concilio -vaticano-ii.html.

Selected Bibliography

CHURCH DOCUMENTS

Acta Synodalia Sacrosancti Concilii Oecumenici Vaticani II. 32 vols. Vatican City: Typis Polyglottis Vaticanis, 1970–99.

Code of Canon Law: Latin-English Edition. Washington, DC: Canon Law Society of America, 1999.

Francis, Pope. "Address during the Apostolic Journey to Rio de Janeiro to the Leadership of the Episcopal Conferences of Latin America during the General Coordination Meeting." https://www.vatican.va/content/francesco/en/speeches/2013/july/documents/papa-francesco_20130728_gmg-celam-rio.html.

———. "Apostolic Exhortation *Evangelii Gaudim* [The Joy of the Gospel]." November 24, 2013. https://www.vatican.va/content/francesco/en/apost_exhortations/documents/papa-francesco_esortazione-ap_20131124_evangelii-gaudium.html.

———. "Christmas Address to the Roman Curia." December 21, 2013. https://www.vatican.va/content/francesco/en/speeches/2013/december/documents/papa-francesco_20131221_auguri-curia-romana.html.

———. "Christmas Address to the Roman Curia." December 22, 2014. https://www.vatican.va/content/francesco/en/speeches/2014/december/documents/papa-francesco_20141222_curia-romana.html.

————. "Christmas Greetings to the Roman Curia." December 22, 2016. https://www.vatican.va/content/francesco/en/speeches/2016/december/documents/papa-francesco_20161222_curia-romana.html.

————. "Christmas Address to the Roman Curia." December 21, 2020. https://www.vatican.va/content/francesco/en/speeches/2020/december/documents/papa-francesco_20201221_curia-romana.html.

————. "Discourse to the Curia. Christmas Greetings for the Roman Curia." December 22, 2014. https://www.vatican.va/content/francesco/en/speeches/2014/december/documents/papa-francesco_20141222_curia-romana.html.

————. "Letter to the People of God." August 20, 2018. https://www.vatican.va/content/francesco/en/letters/2018/documents/papa-francesco_20180820_lettera-popolo-didio.html.

————. Morning Meditation. "L'acqua che scorre nella chiesa." November 9, 2013. https://www.vatican.va/content/francesco/it/cotidie/2013/documents/papa-francesco-cotidie_20131109_acqua-della-grazia.html.

————. "Opening of the XV Ordinary General Assembly of the Synod of Bishops. Address at the Opening of the Synod of Bishops on Young People, the Faith and Vocational Discernment." October 3, 2018. https://www.vatican.va/content/francesco/en/speeches/2018/october/documents/papa-francesco_20181003_apertura-sinodo.html.

————. "Speech at the Commemoration of the 50th Anniversary of the Institution of the Synod of Bishops." October 17, 2015. https://www.vatican.va/content/francesco/en/speeches/2015/october/documents/papa-francesco_20151017_50-anniversario-sinodo.html.

International Theological Commission. "Synodality in the Life and Mission of the Church." March 2, 2018. https://www.vatican.va/roman_curia/congregations/cfaith/cti_documents/rc_cti_20180302_sinodalita_en.html.

Selected Bibliography

Paul VI, Pope. "Address during the Last General Meeting of the Second Vatican Council." December 7, 1965. https://www.vatican.va/content/paul-vi/en/speeches/1965/documents/hf_p-vi_spe_19651207_epilogo-concilio.html.

———. "Apostolic Letter Issued Motu proprio *Apostolica Sollicitudo* [Apostolic Concern]." September 15, 1965. https://www.vatican.va/content/paul-vi/en/motu_proprio/documents/hf_p-vi_motu-proprio_19650915_apostolica-sollicitudo.html.

———. "Apostolic Letter Issued Motu proprio *Sollicitudo Omnium Ecclesiarum* [Care of All]." June 24, 1969. https://www.vatican.va/content/paul-vi/it/motu_proprio/documents/hf_p-vi_motu-proprio_19690624_sollicitudo-omnium-ecclesiarum.html.

———. "Opening speech at Vatican II Second Session." September 29, 1963. https://www.vatican.va/content/paul-vi/it/speeches/1963/documents/hf_p-vi_spe_19630929_concilio-vaticano-ii.html.

———. "Speech at the Beginning of Labors in the Synodal Hall." *Synodus Episcoporum.* September 30, 1967. https://www.vatican.va/content/paul-vi/it/speeches/1967/september/documents/hf_p-vi_spe_19670930_inizio-lavori-sinodo.html.

Schemata Constitutionum et Decretorum de quibus disceptabitur in Concilii sessionibus: De Ecclesia et de B. Maria Virgine. Part 2. Vatican City: Typis Polyglottis Vaticanis, 1962.

Second Vatican Council. Dogmatic Constitution on the Church *Lumen Gentium* [Light of the Nations]. December 7, 1965. Holy See. https://www.vatican.va/archive/hist_councils/ii_vatican_council/documents/vat-ii_const_19641121_lumen-gentium_en.html.

BOOKS

Aymans, Winfried. *Diritto canonico e comunione ecclesiale. Saggi di diritto canonico in prospecttiva theologica.* Torino: Giappichelli Editore, 1993.

SYNODALITY

Battocchio, Riccardo, and Livio Tonello, eds. *Sinodalità: Dimensione della Chiesa, pratiche nella Chiesa*. Padova: EMP, 2020.

Battocchio, Riccardo, and Serena Noceti. *Chiesa e Sinodalità*. Milano: Glossa, 2007.

Bergoglio, Jorge Mario. *Letters of Tribulation*. Edited by Antonio Spadaro, SJ, and Diego Fares. Maryknoll, NY: Orbis Books, 2019.

CELAM. *Renovación y reestructuración del CELAM: Documento de Trabajo*. Bogotá: Celam Press, 2021.

Chapman, Mark D., and Vladimir Latinovic, eds. *Changing the Church: Transformations of Christian Belief, Practice, and Life*. Switzerland: Palgrave MacMillan, 2020.

Compte, María Teresa, and Rafael Luciani, eds. *En camino hacia una Iglesia Sinodal: de Pablo VI a Francisco*. Madrid: PPC, 2020.

Congar, Yves. *Por una Iglesia Servidora y Pobre*. Salamanca: San Esteban, 2014.

————. *True and False Reform in the Church*. Collegeville, MN: Liturgical Press, 1950/2011.

De Smedt, Emile-Joseph. *The Priesthood of the Faithful*. New York: Paulist Press, 1962.

Dianich, Severino. *Diritto e teologia. Ecclesiologia e canonistica per una riforma della Chiesa*. Bologna: EDB, Bologna, 2015.

————. *Riforma della Chiesa e ordinamento canónico*. Bologna: EDB, 2018.

Dianich, Severino, and Serena Noceti. *Trattato sulla Chiesa*. Brescia: Queriniana, 2002.

Duch, Lluís. *Educación y crisis de la modernidad*. Barcelona: Paidós, 1997.

Dulles, Avery. *Church and Society: The Laurence J. McGinley Lectures, 1988–2007*. New York: Fordham University Press, 2008.

Faggioli, Massimo, and Andrea Vicini, eds. *The Legacy of Vatican II*. Mahwah, NJ: Paulist Press 2015.

Fegert, Jörg, Michael Kölch, Elisa König, et al., eds. *Schutz vor sexueller Gewalt und Übergriffen in Institutionen*. Ulm: Springer, Universitäts Klinkum, 2018.

Selected Bibliography

Finucane, Daniel J. *Sensus Fidelium: The Use of a Concept in the Post–Vatican II Era*. Eugene, OR: Wipf & Stock, 1996/2016.

Galli, Carlos M., and Antonio Spadaro, SJ, eds. *For a Missionary Reform of the Church: The Civiltà Cattolica Seminar*. Mahwah, NJ: Paulist Press, 2017.

————. *La riforma e le riforme nella Chiesa*. Brescia: Queriniana, 2016.

Hünermann, Peter, and Bernd Jochen Hilberath, eds. *Herders Theologischer Kommentar zum Zweiten Vatikanischen Konzil*. Vol. 2. Freiburg: Herder, 2004.

Luciani, Rafael, and María del Pilar Silveira, eds. *La sinodalidad en la vida de la Iglesia: Reflexiones para contribuir a la reforma eclesial*. Madrid: San Pablo, 2020.

————. *Pope Francis and the Theology of the People*. Maryknoll, NY: Orbis Books, 2017.

Luciani, Rafael, and Carlos Schickendantz, eds. *Reforma de estructuras y conversión de mentalidades. Retos y desafíos para una Iglesia Sinodal*. Madrid: KHAF, 2020.

Madrigal Terrazas, Jesús Santiago. *Unas lecciones sobre el Vaticano II y su legado*. Madrid: San Pablo, 2012.

Muñoz, Ronaldo. *Nueva conciencia de la Iglesia en América Latina*. Salamanca: Sígueme, 1974.

Noceti, Serena, and Roberto Repole, eds. *Commentario ai documenti del Vaticano II*. Vol. 2. Bologna: EDB, 2015.

Philips, Gérard. *La Iglesia y su misterio en el Concilio Vaticano II: Historia y comentario de la Constitución Lumen Gentium*. Vol. 1. Barcelona: Herder, 1968.

Pié-Ninot, Salvador. *La sacramentalidad de la comunidad cristiana*. Salamanca: Cristiandad, 2007.

Portillo Daniel, ed. *Tolerancia Cero*. México-Madrid: CEPROME-PPC, 2019.

Rahner, Karl. *The Shape of the Church to Come*. London: SPCK, 1974.

————. *Strukturwandel der Kirche als Aufgabe und Chance*. Freiburg-Basel-Wien: Herder, 1972.

Rahner, Karl, and Joseph Ratzinger. *Episcopado y primado*. Barcelona: Herder, 1961/2005.

Rivella, Mauro. *Partecipazione e corresponsabilità nella Chiesa*. Milano: Ancora, 2000.

Scannone, J. C., et al. *Iglesia universal. Iglesias particulares*. Buenos Aires: San Pablo, 2000.

Suenens, León Joseph. *Coresponsibility in the Church*. New York: Herder and Herder, 1968.

Trigo, Pedro. *Concilio Plenario Venezolano: Una constituyente para nuestras Iglesia*. Caracas: Centro Gumilla, 2009.

Vitali, Dario. *Lumen Gentium: Storia, Commento, Recezione*. Rome: Studium, 2012.

ARTICLES

Arrieta, Juan Ignacio. "Órganos de participación y corresponsabilidad en la Iglesia diocesana." *Ius Canonicum* 34, no. 68 (1994).

Bayona Aznar, Bernardo. "Nacimiento, letargo y renacimiento de la colegialidad en el Concilio Vaticano II." *Didaskalia* 45, no. 1 (2015): 117–34.

Beal, John P. "Consultation in Church Governance: Taking Care of Business by Taking After Business." *Canon Law Society of America. Proceedings* 68 (2006): 25–54.

Becquart, XMCJ, Nathalie. "The Synod on Young People, a Laboratory of Synodality." *International Bulletin of Mission Research* (2020). https://journals.sagepub.com/doi/full/10.1177/2396939320951566.

Borras, Alphonse. "Trois expressions de la synodalité depuis Vatican II." *Ephemerides Theologicae Lovanienses* 90, no. 4 (2014).

———. "*Votum tantum consultivum*. Les limites ecclesiologiques d'une formule canonique." *Didaskalia* 45, no. 1 (2015).

Congar, Yves. "The Church: The People of God." *Concilium* 1, no. 1 (1965): 7–36.

———. "Quod omnes tangit ab omnibus tractari et opprobari debet." *Revue historique de droit français et étranger* 36 (1958): 210–59.

———. "Renovación del espíritu y reforma de la institución." *Concilium* 73 (1972): 326–37.

Fernández, Víctor Manuel. "El sensus populi: la legitimidad de una teología desde el pueblo." *Teología* 72 (1998).

Fornés, Juan. "Notas sobre el 'Duo sunt genera Christianorum' del Decreto de Graciano." *Ius Canonicum* 30, no. 60 (1990): 607–32.

Francis, Pope. Interview with Antonio Spadaro, SJ. "Clericalism—That Desire to Lord It Over Lay People—Signifies an Erroneous and Destructive Separation of the Clergy, a Type of Narcissism." *L'Osservatore Romano*, 45, no. 39, September 27, 2013.

———. "The Sovereignty of the People of God. Meeting of the Pope with the Jesuits of Mozambique and Madagascar." *La Civilta Cattolica*, September 5, 2019. https://www.laciviltacattolica.com/the-sovereignty-of-the-people-of-god-the-pontiff-meets-the-jesuits-of-mozambique-and-madagascar/.

Franck, Bernard. "Les expériences synodales après Vatican II." *Communio* 3, no. 3 (1978).

Gera, Lucio. "Puebla: evangelización de la cultura," *Teología* 16, no. 33 (1979).

Legrand, Hervé. "L'articolazione tra le Chiese locali, Chiese regionali e Chiesa universale." *Ad gentes: teologia e antropologia della missione* 3, no. 1 (1999).

———. "Lo sviluppo di chiese-soggetto: un'istanza del Vaticano II." *Cristianesimo nella Storia* 2, no. 1 (1981).

Luciani, Rafael. "Lo que afecta a todos debe ser tratado y aprobado por todos: Hacia estructuras de participación y poder de decisión compartido." *Revista CLAR* 58, no. 1 (2020): 59–66.

———. "Medellín como acontecimiento sinodal: Una eclesialidad colegiada fecundada y completada." *Revista Horizontes* 50 (2018): 482–516.

———. "Medellín Fifty Years Later: From Development to Liberation." *Theological Studies* 79, no. 3 (2018): 566–89.

Parra, SJ, Alberto. "El proceso de sacerdotalización. Una histórica interpretación de los ministerios eclesiales." *Theologica Xaveriana* 28, no. 1 (1978).

Roncagliolo, Cristián. "Iglesia en salida: una aproximación teológico pastoral al concepto de Iglesia en Evangelii Gaudium." *Teología y Vida* 55, no. 2 (2014).

Routhier, Gilles. "Évangilie et modèle de sociabilité." *Laval Théologique et Philosophique* 51, no. 1 (1995).

————. "La synodalitè dans l'Église locale." *Scripta Theologica* 48, no. 3 (2016).

Schickendantz, Carlos. "Estudios sistemático-hermenéuticos sobre el Vaticano II: Tres aportes relevantes en el período posconciliar." *Veritas* 30 (2014): 187–211.

Suenens, Cardinal Léon-Joseph. Interview: "La unidad de la Iglesia en la lógica del Vaticano II: El cardenal Suenens contesta las preguntas de José Broucker." *El Ciervo* 18, no. 184 (1969). https://www.jstor.org/stable/40803679.

ONLINE RESOURCES

"The Causes and Context of Sexual Abuse of Minors by the Catholic Church in the United States between 1950–2010." 87.91.92. Study by John Jay College of Criminal Justice of City University of New York at the request of the U.S. Catholic Bishops' Conference, 2002. https://www.lib.latrobe.edu.au/research/ageofinquiry/biogs/E000235b.htm.

Francis, Pope. Video message October 8, 2020. https://www.vaticannews.va/es/papa/news/2020-10/video-papa.html.

Royal Commission into Institutional Responses to Child Sexual Abuse. "Religious Institutions." In *Final Report*. Canberra: Commonwealth of Australia, 2017. https://www.childabuseroyalcommission.gov.au/final-report.

"Sexueller Missbrauch an Minderjährigen durch katholische Priester, Diakone und männliche Ordensangehörige im Bereich der Deutschen Bischofskonferenz." Mannheim-Heidelberg-Giessen, September 2018. https://bistumlimburg.de/fileadmin/redaktion/Bereiche/missbrauch/MHG-Studie-gesamt.pdf.

ADDITIONAL RESOURCES ON SYNODALITY
Books

Aymans, Winfried. *Das Synodale Element in der Kirchenverfassung.* München: Max Hueber Verlag, 1970.

Borras, Alphonse. *Communion Ecclésiale et Synodalité.* Paris: Éditions CLD, 2019.

Calabrese, Gianfranco. *Ecclesiologia Sinodale.* Bologna: EDB, 2021.

Chapman, Mark D., and Vladimir Latinovic, eds. *Changing the Church: Transformations of Christian Belief, Practice, and Life.* New York: Palgrave MacMillan, 2020.

Comblin, José. *People of God.* Maryknoll, NY: Orbis Books, 2004.

Compte, María Teresa, and Rafael Luciani, eds. *En camino hacia una Iglesia Sinodal: de Pablo VI a Francisco.* Madrid: PPC, 2020.

Congar, Yves. *De la Communion des Églises à une Ecclésiologie de l'Église Universelle.* Paris: Editions du Cerf, 1962.

Gaillardetz, Richard R. *By What Authority? Foundations for Understanding Authority in the Church.* Collegeville, MN: Liturgical Press, 2018.

Graulich, Marcus, and Johanna Rahner, eds. *Synodalität in der Katholischen Kirche.* Freiburg: Herder, 2020.

Hinze, Bradford E. "Synodality and Democracy: For We the People." In *Vaticanum 21: Die bleibenden Aufgaben des Zweiten Vatikanischen Konzils im 21*, edited by Christoph Böttigheimer. Jahrhundert: Dokumentationsband zum Münchner Kongress "Das Konzil 'eröffnen.'" Freiburg im Breisgau, Herder, 2016.

Hünermann, Peter. "Auntorität und Synodalität. Eine Gründfrage der Ekklesiologie." In *Autorität und Synodalität. Eine interdisziplinäre und interkonfessionelle Umschan nach ökumenischen Chancen und ekklesiogischen Desideraten*, edited by C. Böttigheimer and J. Hoffman, 321–48. Frankfurt: O. Lembeck, 2008.

Kelly, Thomas, and Bob Pennington. *Bridge Building: Pope Francis' Practical Theological Approach.* New York: Crossroad, 2020.

Komonchak, Joseph A. "Theological Perspectives on the Exercise of Synodality." In *Il Sinodo dei Vescovi al servizio di una Chiesa sinodale*, edited by Lorenzo Baldisseri. Città del Vaticano: Libreria Editrice Vaticana, 2016.

Luciani, Rafael. "La renovación en la jerarquía eclesial por sí misma no genera la transformación. Situar la colegialidad al interno de la sinodalidad." In *Teología y prevención: Estudio sobre los abusos sexuales en la Iglesia*, edited by Daniel Portillo, 37–64. Santander: Sal Terrae, 2020.

Mayer, Anne Marie C., ed. *The Letter and the Spirit on the Forgotten Documents of Vatican II*. Leuven: Peeters, 2018.

Meloni, Alberto, and Silvia Scatena, eds. *Synod and Synodality: Theology, History, Canon Law and Ecumenism*. Münster: LIT Verlag, 2005.

Pope, Stephen, ed. *Common Calling: The Laity and Governance of the Catholic Church*. Washington, DC: Georgetown University Press, 2004.

Repole, Roberto. *La Chiesa e il suo dono*. Brescia: Queriniana, 2019.

Routhier, Gilles, and Joseph Famerée. *Penser la réforme de l'Église*. Paris: Editions du Cerf, 2021.

Ruggieri, Giuseppe. *Chiesa Sinodale*. Roma: Laterza, 2017.

Sartorio, Ugo. *Sinodalità*. Milano: Ancora 2021.

Szabó, Peter, ed. *Primacy and Synodality: Deepening Insights. Proceedings of the 23rd Congress of the Society for the Law of the Eastern Churches, Debrecen, September 3–8, 2017*. Kanon XXV. Nyíregyháza: St. Athanasius Greek-Catholic Theological Institute, 2019.

Tillard, Jean-Marie R. *Church of Churches: The Ecclesiology of Communion*. Collegeville, MN: Liturgical Press, 1992.

Articles

Antón, Angel. "Strutture sinodali dopo il Concilio. Sinodo dei vescovi, Conferenze Episcopali." *Credere Oggi* 13, no. 4 (1993): 85–105.

Selected Bibliography

Arderí, Raúl. "Una experiencia sinodal en la Iglesia cubana." *Razón y Fe* 283, no. 1451 (2021): 303–13.

Azcuy, Virginia. "The Tensions in the Church Today: Four Fundamental Challenges." *Concilium* 4 (2018): 47–58.

Beal, John P. "The Exercise of the Power of Governance by Lay People: State of the Question." *Jurist* 55, no. 1 (1995): 1–92.

Borras, Alphonse. "La Conférence ecclésiale de l'Amazonie: une institution synodale inédite." *Ephemerides Theologicae Lovanienses* 97, no. 2 (2021): 223–92.

———. "Episcopalis Communio, mérites et limites d'une réforme institutionnelle." *Nouvelle Revue Théologique* 141 (2019): 66–88.

Clifford, Catherine E. "Emerging Consensus on Collegiality and Catholic Ecumenical Responsibility." *Jurist* 64 (2004): 332–60.

Coda, Piero. "The Way of the Church in the Third Millenium." *Proche-Orient Chrétien* 68, nos. 3–4 (2018): 316–25.

Consuelo Vélez, Olga. "Teología feminista latinoamericana de la liberación." *Horizonte* 32 (2013): 1801–12.

Duffy, Eugene. "Processes for Communal Discernment: Diocesan Synods and Assemblies." *Jurist* 71 (2011): 77–90.

Galli, Carlos María. "Constitución de la Conferencia Eclesial de la Amazonía Fundamentos históricos, teológicos, culturales y pastorales." *Revista Medellín* 179 (2020): 517–42.

Haers, Jacques. "A Synodal Process on Synodality: Synodal Missionary Journeying and Common Apostolic Discernment." *Louvain Studies* 43 (2020): 215–38.

Kasper, Walter. "Petrine Ministry and Synodality." *Jurist* 66 (2006): 298–309.

Komonchak, Joseph, A. "The Local Church and the Church Catholic: The Contemporary Theological Problematic." *Jurist* 52 (1992): 416–47.

———. "People of God, Hierarchical Structure, and Communion: An Easy Fit?" *Canon Law Society of America. Proceedings of the Sixteenth Annual Convention* 60 (1998): 91–102.

185

————. "The Status of the Faithful in the Revised Code of Canon Law." *Concilium* 147 (1981): 37–45.

————. "The Synod of 1985 and the notion of the Church." *Chicago Studies* 26 (1987): 330–45.

Legrand, Hervé. "Reception, *Sensus Fidelium*, and Synodal Life: An Effort at Articulation." *Jurist* 57 (1997): 405–31.

————. "La sinodalità, dimensione inerente allá vita ecclesiale: Fondamienti ed attualità." *Vivens Homo* 15 (2005): 5–42.

Luciani, Rafael. "The Centrality of the People in Pope Francis' Sociocultural Theology." *Concilium* 3 (2018): 55–68.

————. "*Hacia una eclesialidad sinodal.*" *Revista Horizontes* 59 (2021).

————. "Medellín as Synodal Event: The Genesis and Development of a Collegial Ecclesiality." *Studia Canonica* 53, no. 1 (2019): 183–208.

————. "Reconfigurar la identidad y la estructura eclesial a la luz de las Iglesias locales. Querida Amazonia y el estatuto teológico de las realidades socioculturales." *Revista Medellín* 46, no. 179 (2020): 487–515.

Madrigal Terrazas, Jesús Santiago. "La conversión del papado en una Iglesia sinodal." *Medellín* 43, no. 168 (2017): 313–31.

————. "Sínodo es nombre de Iglesia. Corresponsabilidad, autoridad y participación." *Sal Terrae* 89, no. 1043 (2001): 197–212.

Mayer, Anne Marie C. "For a Synodal Church: Equipping the Catholic Church on Her Way into the Third Millennium." *Louvain Studies* 43 (2020): 205–14.

Noceti, Serena. "*Sensus fidelium* e dinamiche ecclesiali." *Marriage, Families and Spirituality* 23, no. 1 (2017): 86–98.

————. "What Structures Are Needed for a Reform of the Church?" Concilium 4 (2018): 85–91.

Ombres, Robert. "The Synod of Bishops: Canon Law and Ecclesial Dynamics." *Ecclesiastical Law Journal* 16, no. 3 (2014): 306–18.

Oshaim, Amanda. "Stepping toward a Synodal Church." *Theological Studies* 80 (2019): 370–92.

Selected Bibliography

Pottmeyer, Hermann J. "The Plena et Suprema Potestatis Jurisdictionis of the Pope at the First Vatican Council and Receptio." *Jurist* 57 (1997): 216–34.

Rahner, SJ, Karl. "Towards a Fundamental Theological Interpretation of Vatican II." *Theological Studies* 40, no. 4 (1979): 716–27.

Renken, John A. "Synodality: A Constitutive Element of the Church. Reflections on Pope Francis and Synodality." *Studia Canonica* 52, no. 1 (2018): 5–44.

Routhier, Gilles. "La synodalitè dans l'Église locale." *Scripta Theologica* 48 (2016): 687–706.

Rush, Ormond. "Inverting the Pyramid: The Sensus Fidelium in a Synodal Church." *Theological Studies* 78, no. 2 (2017): 299–325.

———. "*Sensus Fidei*: Faith Making Sense of Revelation." *Theological Studies* 62, no. 2 (2001): 231–61.

Scannone, Juan Carlos. "Pope Francis and the Theology of the People." *Theological Studies* 77 (2016): 118–35.

Schickendantz, Carlos. "Fracaso institucional de un modelo teológico-cultural de Iglesia. Factores sistémicos en la crisis de los abusos." *Teología y Vida* 60 (2019): 9–40.

———. "La reforma de la Iglesia en clave sinodal." *Teología y Vida* 58 (2017): 35–60.

Schmiedl, Joachim. "Es braucht einen neuen Dialog: Theologen und Bischöfe entdecken das Prinzip der Synodalität." *Herder Korrespondenz* 70, no. 4 (2016): 48–49.

———. "Synodalität. Eine Perspektive für die katholische Kirche." *Lebendige Seelsorge* 69, no. 4 (2018): 234–38.

Szabó Péter. "Episcopal Conferences, Particular Councils, and the Renewal of Inter-Diocesan 'Deliberative Synodality.'" *Studia Canonica* 53, no. 1 (2019): 265–96.

Vitali, Dario. "Sensus fidelium e opinione pubblica nella Chiesa." *Gregorianum* 82 (2001): 689–717.

Wijlens, Myriam. "Exercising Collegiality in a Supra-national or Continental Institution Such as the FABC, CCEE, and ComECE." *Jurist* 64 (2004):168–204.

SYNODALITY

———. "Reforming the Church by Hitting the Reset Button: Reconfiguring Collegiality within Synodality because of Sensus Fidei Fidelium." *The Canonist* 8 (2017): 235–61.

———. "Representation and Witnessing in Synodal Structures. Rethinking the Munus Docendi of Episcopal Conferences in Light of Communio Fidelium, Communio Ecclesiarum and Communio Episcoparum." *Studia Canonica* 53 (2019): 75–105.